ROUTLEDGE LIBRARY EDITIONS: 17TH CENTURY PHILOSOPHY

Volume 9

I0592947

THE OLDEST BIOGRAPHY OF SPINOZA

THE OLDEST BIOGRAPHY
OF SPINOZA

EDITED AND TRANSLATED BY
A. WOLF

Routledge
Taylor & Francis Group

LONDON AND NEW YORK

First published in 1927 by Allen & Unwin

This edition first published in 2020
by Routledge
2 Park Square, Milton Park, Abingdon, Oxon OX14 4RN

and by Routledge
52 Vanderbilt Avenue, New York, NY 10017

*Routledge is an imprint of the Taylor & Francis Group, an informa
business*

© 1927 Abraham Wolf
This is a translation of La Vie de feu Monsieur de Spinoza or "La vie
de Spinosa" by Jean Maximilien Lucas (1719)

British Library Cataloguing in Publication Data
A catalogue record for this book is available from the British Library

ISBN: 978-0-367-27875-5 (Set)
ISBN: 978-0-429-29844-8 (Set) (ebk)
ISBN: 978-0-367-18015-7 (Volume 9) (hbk)
ISBN: 978-0-367-18016-4 (Volume 9) (pbk)
ISBN: 978-0-429-05912-4 (Volume 9) (ebk)

Publisher's Note
The publisher has gone to great lengths to ensure the quality of this
reprint but points out that some imperfections in the original copies
may be apparent.

Disclaimer
The publisher has made every effort to trace copyright holders and
would welcome correspondence from those they have been unable to
trace.

THE OLDEST BIOGRAPHY

OF

SPINOZA

EDITED

WITH TRANSLATION, INTRODUCTION,

ANNOTATIONS, ETC.

BY

A. WOLF

PROFESSOR IN THE UNIVERSITY OF LONDON

LONDON

GEORGE ALLEN & UNWIN LTD.

40 MUSEUM STREET

W.C.

Printed in Great Britain by
Unwin Brothers, Ltd., Woking

" The better we know the spirit and character of anybody, the more easily can we explain his utterances." — SPINOZA, *Tractatus Theologico-Politicus*, Ch. VII.

PREFACE

THE two-hundred-and-fiftieth anniversary of the death of Spinoza, which will be celebrated on February 21st, is probably also the two-hundred-and-fiftieth anniversary of the birth of his oldest biography, to which these pages are chiefly devoted. The publication of this volume may therefore be regarded as a fitting contribution to the international celebrations in memory of one of the greatest of the sons of men. In any case, this biography is the oldest, and it is the only one written by one who knew Spinoza personally, and loved him well, if not always wisely. It is obviously high time for a really reliable edition of it to be readily accessible. But in order to be of service to the wider English-reading public I have also added a Translation, an Introduction, and Annotations, and some of the most important Additional Biographical Matter which was written before the better known but less valuable *Life* by Colerus (1705). One of the most important sources of Spinoza biography is, of course, his *Correspondence*, a new translation of which, together with an

Introduction and a Commentary, will be published in the course of this year.

Should circumstances permit, I propose to publish in the near future a companion volume containing a new translation of Colerus from the Dutch original, and all the remaining material of importance for Spinoza biography.

I wish to express my indebtedness to all previous workers in this field, and especially to the late Professor J. Freudenthal and Dr. W. Meyer.

A. WOLF.

UNIVERSITY OF LONDON,
January 1927.

CONTENTS

ILLUSTRATIONS

SPINOZA
1632–1677

I

INTRODUCTION

INTRODUCTION

§ 1. *The First Biography of Spinoza.*

THERE are only two independent old biographies of Spinoza. The better known of the two is that by Colerus, published in 1705. The less known, but older and more valuable biography is the one usually attributed to Lucas, and which was probably begun in 1677 and finished in 1678, though not published until 1719. Neither of these biographies is all that one could wish it to be ; but each is in its own way a remarkable tribute to the character of Spinoza. Colerus's *Life of Spinoza* was translated into French in 1706, and from French into English in the same year. The English translation has been reprinted several times, and is easily procurable. But the so-called Lucas biography of Spinoza has never before been translated into English, nor in fact has it been possible hitherto to obtain a really reliable text of the original. These pages are intended to fill the gap and, at the same time, to furnish other aids to Spinoza biography.

That there should be some inaccuracies even in the oldest biography of Spinoza (to say nothing about Colerus's and other later biographies) is not surprising if we bear in mind some of the circumstances of the life of Spinoza. He left Amsterdam for good in 1660, at the age of twenty-eight. The remaining sixteen years of his life were passed partly in Rhynsburg, near Leyden (1660–1663), partly in Voorburg, near the Hague (1663–1670), and partly in the Hague (1670–1677). His most devoted friends lived either in or near Amsterdam, and although Spinoza visited his native city occasionally between 1660 and 1676, and corresponded with his friends there, close and constant contact with them was rendered impossible by the distance which divided them after his departure from Amsterdam. When, therefore, Spinoza died on February 21, 1677, there was probably nobody who was qualified to give a reliable account of his whole life. There were some in Amsterdam who knew the early part of the story, and there were some in the Hague who knew the later part of it ; but probably nobody knew the whole story from beginning to end.

Moreover, it was not safe to write about Spinoza in a friendly or respectful manner. In fact, some people who knew better actually went out of their way to throw mud at Spinoza in order to divert suspicion from themselves. The result is that our reliable information about the life of Spinoza is rather meagre. And we must feel all the more grateful for the anonymous *Life of the late Mr. de Spinosa*, which is the oldest attempt at a complete biography of Spinoza, and the only one written by somebody who knew him personally.

§ 2. *The Date of the First Biography.*

From internal evidence it would appear that this earliest *Life of Spinosa* was commenced shortly after Spinoza's death, in 1677, and finished either in 1678 or at latest in 1688. The way in which the title refers to Spinoza ("the late Mr. de Spinosa") speaks strongly in favour of an early date ; the author would not have written in that way a long time after the philosopher's death. Again, the biographer refers to the presence of Prince Condé in Utrecht "at the beginning of the late war," and near the end of the biography he expresses his regret that Spinoza "was not fortunate enough to see the end of the late war." The reference is to the war with France during 1672–1678. Now, another war with France broke out in 1689, and of this later war the biography betrays no knowledge or expectation. It must, therefore, have been completed by 1688 at latest. Moreover, the employment of the present tense in the passage referring to the termination of the war in 1678 and the resumption by the States General of the government of Holland ("When the States General are resuming the government," etc.—see pp. 74, 126) suggests that the concluding part of the *Life of Spinosa* was written at the very time when these events were happening, that is, in 1678. This seems very likely also from the fact that the closing passage of the *Life* consists of a warm appeal to fellow-disciples to whom Spinoza was still a recent and vivid memory.

§ 3. *The Authorship of the First Biography.*

Who was the author of this *Life of Spinosa*? The sustained enthusiasm with which it is written makes it obvious that the author must have been a friend and admirer of Spinoza, even an ardent disciple, if not a particularly wise one. The title-page of the 1735 edition says so explicitly (see pp. 83n., 135n.), and earlier manuscript notes speak to the same purpose. But *who* was he? The answer to this question can only be more or less probable, for the manuscripts are anonymous, and the evidence is not absolutely conclusive.

There are but two claimants to the authorship of the oldest biography, namely, Monsieur de Saint-Glain and Sieur Jean Maximilian Lucas. Both were French refugees living in Holland, and both were journalists among other things. Of the two the claim made on behalf of Lucas appears to be the stronger, and the foremost Spinoza scholars who have made a special study of the subject (Dunin-Borkowski, Freudenthal, Meinsma, Meyer) agree in regarding Lucas as the author of the *Life of the late Mr. de Spinosa*.

The sole evidence in support of the claim made on behalf of Saint-Glain's authorship of the *Life* consists of a manuscript note in the margin of a book published in 1731. The book in question is called *Refutation des Erreurs de Benoit de Spinosa*, par M. De Fenelon, Archevêque de Cambray, par le P. Lami, Benedictin, et par M. le Comte de Boulainvilliers, etc. Under the pretence of a " Refutation " it really contains an account of the life and philosophy of Spinoza —the *Life* being a fusion of the oldest biography and that by Colerus. Now, in a copy of this book in the Royal Library at the Hague, on the page where the book speaks of the French trans-lation of Spinoza's *Tractatus Theologico-Politicus*, which was published in 1678 with the title *La Clef de Sanctuaire*, there is a manuscript note, in the margin, to the following effect : " With regard to the author of this translation opinions are divided. Some attribute it to the late Mr. de Saint-Glain, author of the *Gazette of Rotterdam* [really *Amsterdam*], others to Mr. Lucas, author of the *Quintessence* ; but it is quite certain that it is by the same person who wrote the *Life of de Spinosa*. Bibl. Raison., t. 7. p. 169." The first part of this note, referring to the French translation of the *Tractatus Theologico-Politicus*, only reproduces what is said in both of the 1719 editions of the *Life of Spinosa* (see pp. 84, 136). The rest is new. If it were true that the *Life* and the translation had the same author, then Saint-Glain's claim would be very strong, for both of the 1719 editions seem to leave little doubt that Saint-Glain was the translator of the *Tractatus Theologico-Politicus* into French. And if Saint-Glain really was the author of the *Life of Spinosa*, then we have an additional datum for determining its date. For it is known that Saint-Glain died on January 18, 1685,* so that he must have finished the *Life* in 1684 at the latest, if he wrote it at all. It certainly is remarkable that the catalogue of books given at the end of the Le Vier edition of the *Life* (see pp. 87 ff., 139 ff.) contains nothing that was published later than

* P. Bayle : *Œuvres Diverses,* vol. iv, p. 616.

1684. On the other hand, Saint-Glain may only have been the " other disciple " who compiled the Catalogue (see pp. 83n., 135n.). Or, again, Lucas may have written both the *Life* and the Translation. On the whole, it is perhaps unreasonable to allow such a late marginal note to upset other and earlier evidence in support of Saint-Glain's authorship of the French translation of the *Tractatus Theologico-Politicus*, and of Lucas's authorship of the *Life of Spinosa*.

The evidence in favour of Lucas's authorship of the *Life* is much stronger than that in favour of Saint-Glain's authorship. In both editions of the *Life of Spinosa* which were printed in Amsterdam in 1719 there is a Preface (see pp. 81 f., 133 f.) which contains the following remarks : " The author is forsooth unknown, although it is apparent that he who has composed it had been one of his [Spinoza's] Disciples, as he explains very clearly. If, however, it were permitted to build something on conjectures, one might say, and maybe with certainty, that the whole Work was the doing of the late Mr. Lucas, so famous for his *Quintessences*, but even more so for his morals and his mode of life." In a manuscript copy of the *Life* possessed by the Meermanus-Westreenianum, in the Hague, there is a note that it may be regarded " maybe with certainty " that the author was " the late Mr. Lucas, who was a friend and disciple of Mr. de Spinosa." This note must have been written soon after the death of Lucas, which took place on February 22, 1697, almost exactly twenty years after the death of Spinoza. The account of Lucas which follows will afford a little more evidence in support of his claims to the authorship of the *Life of Spinosa*. More conclusive evidence would no doubt be welcome. But having regard to all the circumstances, one may reasonably admit the claims of Lucas with considerable probability.

§ 4. *Lucas.*

Jean Maximilien Lucas was born at Rouen either in 1636 or in 1646, and died at the Hague in 1697. He came of a family of publishers, and was himself a publisher among other things. One of his most interesting publications was a *Reply* (1675) to M. Sorbiere's *Voyage to England* (1664), which latter had caused consternation among the Fellows of the Royal Society, and had provoked a reply also from Dr. Thomas Sprat, the historian of that Society. What exactly brought Lucas from France to Holland is not known for certain, but may be guessed from his

PROBABLE PORTRAIT OF J. M. LUCAS

doings in Holland. For he appears to have devoted much of his energy and substance in conducting a violent campaign against Louis XIV, " le roi soleil " of France. Presumably Lucas and his brother, like Descartes and other distinguished men " turned out " by France, were too independent in thought and free in speech to feel safe in their native country. At that time Holland, notwithstanding its Calvinistic zealots, was the freest country in Europe, and harboured many French and other refugees. Still, even in Holland freedom was limited, and the authorities had to pay some regard to the susceptibilities of the King of France and his proneness to bully his neighbours and make war against them. So Lucas was arrested and fined repeatedly by the Dutch authorities for publishing things offensive to Louis XIV. But Lucas persisted. He conducted in turn various periodicals—the *Gazette de Hollande*, the *Gazette ordinaire d'Amsterdam*, the *Nouvelles Extraordinaires*, and the *Quintessence*. Some of these publications had to be suppressed occasionally in order to pacify the King of France. It was even rumoured that one of the chief reasons for the French invasion of Holland in 1672 was the French King's annoyance with the Dutch authorities for failing to stop effectively Lucas's journalistic campaign against him. But it was during the subsequent war with France, which broke out in 1689, that Lucas made his most violent attacks on Louis XIV. He did this in the columns of the *Quintessence* (or, to give it the full title, *La Quintessence des nouvelles, historiques, critiques, politiques*), through which Lucas became specially notorious.

What is of special interest to students of the *Life of Spinosa* is the fact that it was a subsequent editor of the *Quintessence* who first published the *Life* in the tenth volume of the *Nouvelles litteraires contenant ce qui se passe de plus considerable dans la République des lettres* (Amsterdam, H. du Sauzet, 1719), of which he was also the editor. It looks as if the manuscript of the *Life of Spinosa* had passed from Lucas to each successive editor of the *Quintessence*, until one of them had the courage to print it.

Lucas was a free-thinker, apparently also a Rosicrucian. (The Rosicrucians were in effect the Freemasons of Holland in the seventeenth century.) He is sometimes also described as a doctor (*medicin*), perhaps only by courtesy. He was a man of strong likes and violent dislikes. Perhaps it would be too much to expect discriminating judgment from such a free-lance. If he was the author of the *Life of Spinosa*, he

26

was most probably also the author of the *Spirit of Spinosa*, which follows the *Life* in several manuscripts, and in one of the two editions (the Le Vier edition), printed in 1719. This so-called *Spirit of Spinosa* is a very superficial, tactless, free-thinking treatise, which may betray the spirit of Lucas, but certainly does not show the spirit of Spinoza. It contains an attack on the founders of the three historic religions, and roundly charges all three with having been impostors. When it is recalled with what reverence Spinoza always refers to Christ (although he rejects the idea of a God-Man), and how he insists that human nature should never be ridiculed, but studied, it may be realized how little Lucas had really learned from Spinoza. It also illustrates the kind of thing that tended to bring the name of Spinoza into disrepute. Unfortunately, it is the common fate of great teachers to be betrayed by weak disciples. Lucas would have deserved more if he had written less. But having his *Life*, we may endeavour to forget his *Spirit*.

One more item of interest may be added here before we leave Lucas. Within the same short period of time (according to the researches of the late Dr. W. Meyer) the editor of the *Gazette ordinaire d'Amsterdam* is variously referred to by contemporaries as De la Fond, as Van Swol, and as Lucas. It looks as if, owing to his repeated trouble with the authorities, Lucas assumed several aliases, and that De la Fond was one of them. If so, we may see what Lucas looked like, for a fine etching of De la Fond is still in existence (see portrait).

§ 5. *The First Printed Editions.*

As has already been mentioned incidentally, the *Life of Spinosa*, by Lucas, first appeared in print in 1719. It was published in two forms within the same year. It was printed as an article in the *Nouvelles Litteraires* (vol. x, pp. 40–74), and also in an independent volume together with *L'Esprit de Spinosa*. The article bore the title *La Vie de Spinosa*, the volume *La Vie et l'Esprit de Mr. Benoit de Spinosa*. Both were anonymous, and the volume did not even give the name of the publisher or of the place of publication. But it is known now that the volume was published in Amsterdam by Charles le Vier. The attack on Christianity contained in *L'Esprit de Spinosa* provoked such consternation that both editions were suppressed soon after their publication, and only very few copies have escaped destruction. Of the *Nouvelles Litteraires* edition there are copies in the Göttingen University Library, in Leyden, and in Paris (Bibliothèque Nationale) ; but these are all the known copies. Of the complete Le Vier volume there is a copy in the University Library at Halle-Saale, and another is at present in London ; no other copies are known of. There are, however, some copies of the *Life* alone purporting to have been published in Hamburg in 1735. These copies are really the first part of the complete Le Vier edition re-issued with a new title-page, and a modified preface, and without the table of contents and the *L'Esprit de Spinosa*, to which the table of contents mostly referred. Of this re-issued first part, having for its new title *La Vie de Spinosa par un de ses Disciples*, there are copies in the British Museum, in Leipzig, in Munich, in Paris, in Vienna, and elsewhere.

One result of the scarcity of copies of Lucas's *Life of Spinosa* was that for a long time, in fact until comparatively recently, the biography of Spinoza published by Colerus in 1705 (French and English translations 1706) established itself as the oldest and most authentic account of Spinoza, and it required a great amount of research to put matters right again. How it all happened will become clear from what follows.

§ 6. *Colerus.*

Johann Köhler (latinized *Colerus*) was a German born at Düsseldorf in 1647. In 1679 he went to Amsterdam as Minister of the Lutheran Church there. In 1693 he was transferred to the Lutheran Church at the Hague, where he died in 1707. By a fortunate coincidence his lodgings in the Hague consisted of the same rooms, in a house in the Stille Veerkade, which Spinoza had occupied during 1670–1671. Just round the corner, in the Paviljoensgracht, there still lived the Van der Spycks, with whom Spinoza had lodged during the rest of his life. Apparently the Van der Spycks and others often spoke to him about Spinoza, and so Colerus became interested. The Bible-criticism and the whole philosophy of Spinoza were not likely to meet with any sympathy from Colerus, who (according to Stolle, a German contemporary) was not particularly deep, and so zealous in his orthodoxy that if he had his way with God he would have played the part of more than one Elijah. But he had his good points, and was a favourite with his congregation. In 1705 he published, in Dutch, a treatise *On the True Resurrection of Jesus Christ from the Dead, defended against Spinosa and his followers. Together with a precise biography of the same famous philosopher compiled from his posthumous writings and the oral testimony of trustworthy persons who are still living.* Although the primary purpose of Colerus was to refute Spinoza, that did not blind him to the worth of Spinoza's character. All considered, the biography does Colerus credit. Moreover, appearing under such respectable auspices, this biography did not have the fate of Lucas's *Life of Spinosa*, but on the contrary enjoyed a certain vogue, as is evident from its immediate translation into French and English. It was inevitable, of course, that there should be many inaccuracies in a biography written nearly thirty years after the philosopher's death, and which relied mainly on the reports of old people of moderate education.

All that time the biography written by Lucas could only circulate secretly in a few manuscript copies, and so could have been known to very few only. It was unknown even to Colerus. Now, some of those who did get to know the Lucas biography as well as that by Colerus naturally attempted to piece the two together into one whole. Already the Le Vier edition of 1719 interpolated a long passage from Colerus (see pp. 85 f., 137 f.) ; and Count Boulainvilliers, in the afore-mentioned biography published in 1731, carried this kind of patchwork much further.

One result of this composite method of Spinoza biography was that when at last Spinoza scholars did come across copies of Lucas they noticed the interpolations from Colerus, and concluded that the Lucas biography was later than that by Colerus, from which it seemed to have borrowed. It was only when manuscripts of the original Lucas text were discovered that it became evident that the Lucas biography was absolutely independent of Colerus, and much older and more correct.

7 *The Lucas Manuscripts.*

During the past thirty years or so Spinoza scholars have ransacked European libraries with considerable success. Among other things a number of manuscript copies of the Lucas biography have been unearthed. The libraries at Göttingen, Dresden, and Paris possess two manuscripts each, and the libraries at the Hague, Halle-Saale, Munich, and Vienna have one each. These manuscripts have all been examined by Freudenthal and Dunin-Borkowski with the friendly co-operation of various helpers ; and the most important of them have been examined again by the present writer. The fullest and most reliable account of the collations of the different manuscripts has been published by

THE PAVILJOENSGRACHT, IN THE HAGUE, AS IT LOOKED FORMERLY

Dunin-Borkowski in the *Archiv für Geschichte der Philosophie* (vol. xviii, 1904), and a summary is also given in his *Der Junge De Spinoza* (1910). The main conclusion arrived at is that the best of the then known manuscripts, that is the one which gives a text most like the original Lucas biography, is the Paris manuscript, Codex No. 2235, in the Bibliothèque de l'Arsenal. Codex No. 2236, in the same library, is very similar, but later. Both manuscripts bear the title : *La Metaphysique et l'Ethique de Spinosa, son Esprit et sa Vie.* And both contain, in addition to Lucas's *La Vie et l'Esprit de Spinosa*, also the essay which Boulainvilliers wrote in 1712, and published in 1731 in the so-called *Refutation* already referred to above. These two manuscripts are usually described as Codex A and Codex A¹ respectively.

Since the publication of the results of Dunin-Borkowski's researches another important Lucas manuscript has come to light in London. For reasons to be explained presently, it will be described as Codex Towneley, or Codex T for short.

§ 8. *Codex Towneley.*

This manuscript is a small quarto volume containing 191 pages written in a very neat

c   33

hand. The first 51 pages contain *La Vie de feu Monsieur de Spinosa*, then come three blank leaves, which are followed by 140 pages, written in the same hand, but paginated separately, of *L'Esprit*. In front of *La Vie* and also of *L'Esprit* there is a pen-and-ink sketch showing a hand pointing from the clouds to a volume inscribed *B. D. S. Ces Paroles sont Esprit et Vie*, while under the sketch are some flattering rhymes about the immortality of the works of Spinoza (see the illustration facing page 40, and facsimile of the first page of the text facing page 96). The second part has not got the title *L'Esprit de Spinosa*, but begins straightway with the chapter-heading, *De Dieu*.

This manuscript appears to me to be both older and better than any other Lucas manuscript discovered hitherto. It has nearly all the good points of Codex A and others besides ; though it also has at least one odd mistake (*Hebden* for *Enden*, see pp. 52 n., 104 n.).

The text of *La Vie de feu Monsieur de Spinosa* which is printed in this volume is based on Codex T and collated with Codex A, which is the most important of the other manuscripts.

The story of the Towneley Codex has not yet been completely ascertained. The most important clue to it consists of a book-plate inside the front cover. It is the book-plate of *John Towneley*, *Esq.*, and has the motto (*Tenes le Vraye*) and the arms (three mullets, etc.) of the Towneleys of Towneley Hall, Lancs. According to the *Dictionary of National Biography*, John Towneley (the son of Charles Towneley, of Towneley Hall, Lancs) was born in 1697, and died in 1782. He was in Paris in 1728, held a commission in Rothes's Franco-Irish Infantry Regiment from 1731 onwards, and distinguished himself at the siege of Philippsburg in 1734. His intelligence and general knowledge were favourably spoken of by the French envoy, the Marquis d'Eguilles, in 1746. He rendered *Hudibras* into French. Clearly a man of wide interests. The suggestion lies to hand that he probably picked up the manuscript in France or in the Low Countries. The sale catalogue of his library (*Bibliotheca Towneleiana*, 1814 and 1815) shows that he was a collector of books and manuscripts. Unfortunately, I cannot find any mention of the Lucas manuscript in that catalogue. But there was a long interval between the sale of the library and the death of its owner, during which, or already in his lifetime, the manuscript may have been disposed of. Or it may have been included in one of the groups of manuscripts which were sold in " lots."

§ 9. *Select Literature of Spinoza Biography.*

The following select bibliography is intended as a start for the student of the life and character of Spinoza. For the adequate understanding of his philosophy much more is required, of course, than a knowledge of his biography. But of Spinoza it is probably more true than of any other philosopher that his thought cannot be divorced from his life and character without grave risks of total misapprehension.

BALTZER (A.) : *Spinozas Entwicklungsgang, besonders nach seinen Briefen geschildert,* 1888.

DUNIN-BORKOWSKI (S. VON) : *Der junge De Spinoza. Leben und Werdegang im Lichte der Weltphilosophie,* 1910.

Zur Textgeschichte und Textkritik der ältesten Lebensbeschreibung Benedikt Despinozas, in the *Archiv für Geschichte der Philosophie,* vol. xviii, 1904.

FREUDENTHAL (J.) : *Die Lebensgeschichte Spinozas in Quellenschriften, Urkunden und Nichtamtlichen Nachrichten,* 1899.

Spinoza, sein Leben und seine Lehre, Erster Band, *Das Leben Spinozas,* 1904.

Ueber den Text der Lucasschen Biographie Spinozas in *Zeitschrift für Philosophie,* vol. 126, 1905.

GEBHARDT (C.) : *Spinoza, Lebensbeschreibungen und Gespräche,* 1914.

MEINSMA (K. O.) : *Spinoza en zijn Kring,* 1896, or *Spinoza und sein Kreis,* 1909.

MEYER (W.) : *De Strijd der Refugiës in Holland tegen het Staatsbeleid van Lodewijk XIV* in the *Tijdspiegel,* 1904.

Jean Maximilien Lucas in the *Tijdschrift voor Boek-en Bibliotheekwezen,* 1906.

Archiv für Geschichte der Philosophie, 1898, 1902, 1903.

WOLF (A.) : *Spinoza, His Life and Treatise on God and Man,* 1910.

§ 10. *Note Concerning Text and Translation.*

The *Text* of *La Vie de feu Monsieur de Spinosa* given in this work is based on Codex T. As Codex A is the most valuable and helpful of the other known manuscripts of the Lucas biography, it is the only one with which Codex T is collated in detail in the present edition. Except where there is some indication to the contrary, the text is in accordance with both Codices A and T. When the reading in the two is different, the text gives one of them (usually, but not always, that of T), while a footnote gives the other (usually, though not always, that of A). In the very few cases in which neither manuscript is correct the suggested correct reading is given in the text in *square* brackets, while the actual reading of both manuscripts is put in a footnote. Where a word appears to have been omitted from both codices it is inserted in the text in square brackets without comment. In the case of the *Translation*, only the most important of the different readings are given, as in most cases the *variæ lectiones* (given fully in the French *Text*) make no difference to the meaning. The *numbered* footnotes in the text and the translation are copied from the manuscript.

Strict regard for the documents dealt with has made it impossible to maintain uniformity of spelling. But the variations are not likely to cause any serious trouble.

II

THE LIFE OF
THE LATE MR. DE SPINOSA

Renowned Spinosa's features
No faithful brush portrays,
But, Wisdom being immortal,
His works will live always.*

* This tribute is not in A, nor in the *Nouvelles Litteraires* edition of 1719, nor in the 1735 edition; but it is printed on the title-page of the Le Vier edition of 1719.

PICTORIAL TITLE-PAGE OF THE TOWNELEY MANUSCRIPT

THE LIFE OF THE LATE MR. DE SPINOSA

OUR age is very enlightened, but it is not therefore more just to great men. Although it is indebted to them for its most precious enlightenment, and happily benefits therefrom, yet, whether from envy or from ignorance, it cannot bear that anyone should praise them ; and it is surprising that one should have to conceal himself in order to write their life, as if he were about to commit a crime ; especially is this so if these great men have made themselves famous by views that are unusual and unknown to common souls. For then, under the pretext of doing honour to received opinions, however absurd or ridiculous, they defend their own ignorance, to which they sacrifice the sanest light of reason and, so to say, truth itself. But whatever risk one may run on such a thorny course, I would have profited little indeed from his philosophy whose life and maxims I take upon myself to write, if I were afraid to undertake it. I little fear the fury of the people, as I have the honour to live in a Republic which permits its subjects freedom of opinion, and where it would even be needless to wish to be happy, if people of tried probity would be regarded without jealousy. Even if this work, which I consecrate to the memory of an illustrious friend, be not approved by everybody, it will at least be approved by those who only love Truth and who have a kind of aversion for the impudent mob.

BARUCH DE SPINOSA was born in Amsterdam, the most beautiful city of Europe, and was of very modest origin. For his father, who was a Portuguese Jew, had not the means to help him on in business and therefore decided to let him take up the study of Hebrew Literature. This kind of study, which constitutes the whole of Jewish science, was not capable of satisfying completely a brilliant mind like his. He was not yet fifteen years old when he raised difficulties which the most learned among the Jews found it hard to solve. And although such extreme youth is hardly the age of understanding, still he had enough of it to perceive that his doubts embarrassed his teacher. Being afraid to irritate him, he pretended to be very satisfied with his answers, contenting himself with writing them down in order to make use of them at the proper time and place. As he read nothing but the Bible he soon made himself able to have no further need of an expositor. He made such just comments on it that the Rabbis only answered him after the manner of ignoramuses who, when they see their argument exhausted, charge those who press them too much with having opinions little in harmony with their religion. Such an odd procedure made him realize that it was useless for the purpose of seeking Truth. " The people do not know her. Besides, to trust blindly even the most authentic books," he said, " is to be too fond of old errors." He decided, accordingly, to consult no one but himself in this matter, but to spare no effort in order to discover her. It needed a great mind, and one of extraordinary strength, to conceive, before the age of twenty, a plan of such importance. In fact, he soon made it clear that he had undertaken nothing rashly. For, beginning to read Scripture all over again, he penetrated its obscurity, laid bare its mysteries, and brought daylight athwart the clouds behind which it had been told him that Truth was hidden.

After the examination of the Bible he read and re-read the Talmud with the same closeness. And, as he had not his equal in his knowledge of Hebrew, he found nothing difficult in it, but also nothing satisfying. But he was so judicious that he allowed his thoughts to mature before approving them.

43

In the meantime Morteira, a celebrity among the Jews, and the least ignorant of all the Rabbis of his time, admired the conduct and the genius of his disciple. He could not understand how a young man of such penetration could be so modest. In order to know him through and through he tried him in every way, as he acknowledged when he found nothing to criticize both in his morals and in the fineness of his mind. Morteira's approval, although it enhanced the good opinion which people had of his disciple, did not make him at all vain. Although he was so very young, yet thanks to his prudence he attached little importance to the friendliness and the praises of men. Moreover, the love of Truth was so very much his ruling passion that he scarcely saw anybody. But whatever precaution he took, still there are some encounters which one cannot decently avoid even if they are often dangerous.

Among those who were most eager to associate with him there were two young men who, professing to be his most intimate friends, adjured him to tell them his real views. They represented to him that whatever his opinions were he had nothing to fear on their part, as their curiosity had no other object than to clear up their own doubts. The young disciple, surprised by such an unexpected utterance, did not answer them for some time ; but seeing that he was pressed he told them smiling that they had Moses and the Prophets who were true Israelites, that these had decided about everything, and that they ought to follow them without hesitation if they were truly Israelites. " If one is to believe them," replied one of these young men, " then I do not see that there is any non-material Being, that God has no body, nor that the soul is immortal, nor that the Angels are a real substance. How does it appear to you ? " he continued, addressing himself to our disciple ; " Has God a body ? Are there any Angels ? Is the soul immortal ? " " I confess," said the disciple, " that since nothing is to be found in the Bible about the non-material or incorporeal, there is nothing objectionable in believing that God is a body.* All the more so since, as the Prophet says, God [1] is great, and it is impossible to comprehend greatness without extension and, therefore, without body. As for spirits, it is certain that Scripture does not say that these are real and permanent substances, but mere phantoms, called angels because God makes use of them to declare His will ; they are of such kind that the angels and all other

[1] Psalm xlviii. 1.   * A : a created body.

kinds of spirits are invisible only because their matter is very fine and diaphanous, so that it can only be seen as one sees phantoms in a mirror, in a dream, or in the night ; even as Jacob in his sleep saw angels ascending and descending a ladder. That is why we do not read that the Jews excommunicated the Sadducees who did not believe in Angels because the Old Testament says nothing about their creation. With regard to the soul, wherever Scripture speaks of it the word Soul is used simply to express Life, or anything that is living. It would be useless to search for any passage in support of its immortality. As for the contrary view, it may be seen in a hundred places, and nothing is so easy as to prove it : but this is neither the place nor the time to discuss it." " The little that you have said about it," replied one of the two friends, " should convince the most incredulous, but it is not enough to satisfy your friends, who require something more solid ; besides, the matter is too important to be only touched on. We only leave you now on condition that you resume the subject another time." The disciple, who only sought to break off the conversation, promised them all they wanted, but subsequently evaded all occasions on which they might try to renew it ; and considering that man's curiosity rarely has a good motive, he studied the behaviour of his friends and discovered so much to find fault with, that he broke off all association with them and would not speak to them any more.

His friends, when they perceived what his intention was, contented themselves with murmuring about him to one another so long as they thought that this was only done by him in order to test them, but when they saw that there was no hope of their being able to bend him, then they vowed to take revenge, and in order to do it more sensibly they commenced by depreciating him in the mind of the people. They said that the people deceived themselves in believing that this young man might become one of the pillars of the Synagogue ; that it seemed more likely that he would be its destroyer, as he had nothing but hatred and contempt for the Law of Moses ; that they had frequently visited him, on Morteira's recommendation, but they discovered that he was impious, and that the Rabbi was mistaken in having a good opinion of him ; his very approach caused them horror.

This false rumour, disseminated on the sly, soon became public, and when they saw the proper time to push it more actively they made their report to the Judges of the Synagogue, whom they incited in such a manner that they thought of condemning him without hearing him first. When the ardour of the first flare had passed (the holy ministers of the Temple are not exempt from wrath), they had him summoned to appear before them. On his part, feeling that his conscience had nothing to reproach him, he went cheerfully to the Synagogue, where his Judges, with woe-begone countenance and like men consumed with zeal for the house of God, said to him that, after the great hopes which they had entertained about his piety, they found it difficult to believe the evil rumour that was going round concerning him, that in the bitterness of their heart they had summoned him to give an account of his faith ; that he was accused of the most awful of all crimes, namely, contempt for the Law ; that they ardently wished that he might clear himself of it, but that, if he should be convicted, then there was no torment severe enough for his punishment. They then adjured him to tell them if he were guilty, and when they saw that he denied it, his false friends, who were present, deposed boldly that they had heard him scoff at the Jews as " superstitious people born and bred in ignorance, who do not know what God is, and who nevertheless have the audacity to speak of themselves as His people, to the disparagement of other nations

As for the Law, it was instituted by a man who was forsooth better versed than they were in the matter of Politics, but who was hardly more enlightened than they were in Physics or even in Theology ; with an ounce of good sense one could discover the imposture, and one must be as stupid as the Hebrews of the time of Moses to believe that gallant man."

That, added, by these Libertines, to what he had said about God, the Angels, and the Soul, stirred their spirits and made them cry Anathema at him even before the accused had time to justify himself.

The Judges, impelled by a holy zeal to avenge the profanation of their Law, question him, press him, threaten him. Thereupon the accused retorted that their wry faces made him pity them, that he would admit what they said on the evidence of such good witnesses, if it was not necessary to support it with incontestable reasons.

In the meantime Morteira, having heard of the peril in which his disciple was placed, hastened with long strides to the Synagogue, where, after taking his place with the Judges, he demanded of him : " Whether he was mindful of the good example he had set him ? Whether his rebellion was the fruit * of the pains that he

* A : reward.

had taken with his education ? And if he was not afraid of falling into the hands of the living God ? The scandal was already great, but there was still time for him to repent."

After Morteira had exhausted his rhetoric, without being able to shake the determination of his disciple, then as Chief of the Synagogue he urged him in a most formidable tone to make up his mind for repentance or for punishment, and he vowed that he would excommunicate him if he did not immediately show signs of contrition. Undismayed, the disciple answered him : " That he knew the gravity of his threats, and that, in return for the trouble which he had taken to teach him the Hebrew language, he was quite willing to show him how to excommunicate."

At these words the Rabbi in a passion vented all his spleen against him. After some cold rebukes he dismissed the assembly, left the Synagogue, and vowed not to come there again except with the thunderbolt in his hand. But, whatever the vow which he made, he did not believe that his disciple had the courage to await its fulfilment. He was mistaken in his conjectures, for the sequel showed that, if he was well informed about the fineness of his mind, he was not well informed about its firmness. The time, subsequently taken in order to represent to him in what abyss he was about to throw himself, having passed in vain, a day was appointed for his excommunication. As soon as he heard of it, he prepared himself for retirement, and was so far from being alarmed by it that to the person who brought him the news he said : " All the better ; they do not force me to do anything that I would not have done of my own accord if I did not dread scandal ; but, since they want it that way, I enter gladly on the path that is opened to me, with the consolation that my departure will be more innocent than was the exodus of the early Hebrews from Egypt. Although my subsistence is no better secured than was theirs,[2] I take away nothing from anybody, and, whatever injustice may be done to me, I can boast that people have nothing to reproach me with."

He had so little intercourse with the Jews for some time that he was obliged to associate with Christians, and he formed ties of friendship with intellectual people who told him that it was a pity that he knew neither Greek nor Latin. Although he was well versed in Hebrew, in Italian, and in Spanish, to say nothing of German,

[2] It is said in Exodus xii. 35, 36, that the Hebrews took away from the Egyptians silver and raiment which they had borrowed by the command of Moses.

Flemish, and Portuguese, which were his natural languages, he himself fully realized of what importance it was to find the means of mastering Greek and Latin, as he was not born rich and had no influential friends to help him on.

As he was thinking about it incessantly and spoke of it whenever he met people, Van den Enden,* who taught Greek and Latin with success, offered to look after him and to put him up in his own house without exacting any other return than that he should sometimes help him to instruct his pupils when able to do so.

In the meantime Morteira, irritated by the contempt which his disciple had shown for him and his Law, changed his friendship to hatred, and in launching his thunderbolt at him tasted the pleasure which base souls find in revenge.

The excommunication of the Jews has nothing very peculiar ; still, in order not to omit anything that may instruct the reader, I will now refer to the principal circumstances. When the people have assembled in the synagogue, the ceremony which they call Herim 3 begins with the lighting of a quantity of black wax-candles and the opening of the ark where the books of the Law are kept. Then the precentor, standing on a

3 *Herim* in Hebrew means Separation.
* T : Hebden.

slightly raised place, intones the words of the excommunication in a doleful voice, while another precentor blows a horn,[4] and the wax-candles are turned upside down so as to make them fall drop by drop into a vessel full of blood. Thereupon the people, animated with a holy horror at the sight of the black spectacle, respond Amen in a furious tone, which bears witness to the good service which they believe they would render to God if they could tear the excommunicated to pieces ; as they would do without doubt if they met him at that moment or when leaving the synagogue. In this connection it is to be remarked that the sound of the horn, the reversed wax-candles, and the vessel full of blood are circumstances which are only observed in the case of blasphemy, that otherwise they are content merely to fulminate the excommunication, as was done in the case of Mr. Spinosa, who was not convicted of blasphemy, but only of want of respect for Moses and for the Law.

Excommunication is such a grave matter among the Jews that the best friends of the excommunicated dare not render him any service, or even speak to him, without incurring the same penalty. Therefore those who fear the

4 A Horn is called in Hebrew *Sophar* [*Shophar*].

sweetness of solitude and the impertinence of the people prefer to bear any other penalty rather than the Anathema.

MR. DE SPINOSA, who had found a refuge where he believed himself protected from the insults of the Jews, thought of nothing more than of getting on with the human sciences, in which, with such excellent genius as his, he was able to make very considerable progress in a very short time.

In the meanwhile the Jews, much agitated because their thrust had missed and because he whom they wanted to get rid of was beyond their power, charged him with a crime of which they could not convict him. I speak of the Jews in general, for I dare not say that Morteira and his colleagues were his greatest enemies, true though it is to say that those who obtain their living from the Altar never forgive. To have withdrawn from their jurisdiction and to subsist without their help, these were two crimes which seemed to them unpardonable. Morteira especially could not relish the fact that his disciple and he were staying in the same city after the affront which he thought he had received. But what could he do to drive him out of it ? He was not the Chief of the city as he was of the Synagogue. However, malice in the guise of a feigned zeal is so potent that the old man attained his object, and this is how he achieved it. He got a Rabbi of the same temper to accompany him and went to find the Magistrates, to whom he represented that if he had excommunicated Mr. de Spinosa it was not for ordinary reasons but for execrable blasphemies against Moses and against God. He exaggerated the falsehood by all such arguments as a holy hatred suggests to an irreconcilable heart, and demanded in conclusion that the accused should be banished from Amsterdam. From the behaviour of the Rabbi and the eagerness with which he declaimed against his disciple, it was easy to Judge that it was personal wrath rather than pious zeal that incited him to vengeance. As the Judges perceived this and sought to get away from their complaints, they sent them to the clergy. These, after examining them, found themselves embarrassed. They discerned nothing impious in the way in which the accused had justified himself. On the other hand, the accuser was a Rabbi, and the office which he held made them think of theirs. All well considered they could not, without outrage to the office of clergymen, absolve a man who wanted to overthrow their like, and this reason, good or bad, made them give their decision in favour of the Rabbi. The decision was such that the Magistrates, who for reasons easy to surmise dared not gainsay them, condemned the accused to exile for several months.

In this way Rabbinism was avenged, but it is true that this was not what the Judges directly aimed at so much as the getting rid of the importunate clamours of the most vexatious of all men. For the rest, this sentence, very far from injuring Mr. de Spinosa, favoured the longing which he felt to leave Amsterdam.

Having learnt as much of the human sciences as a philosopher ought to know, he was thinking of freeing himself from the crowd of a large city when they started to worry him. So it was not persecution that drove him thence, but the love of solitude in which, he had no doubt, he would find Truth. This strong passion, which gave him little rest, made him leave with joy his native city for a village called Rhinburg, where, removed from all the obstacles which he could only overcome by flight, he devoted himself entirely to philosophy. As there were few authors who were to his liking, he had recourse to his own meditations, being resolved to ascertain how far they could reach. In this respect he has given such a lofty impression of the greatness of his mind that there are assuredly

56

few persons who have penetrated as far as he did in the subjects of which he has treated.

For two years he stayed in this retreat, where, although he took precautions to avoid all intercourse with his friends, his most intimate friends went to see him from time to time, and only left him again with reluctance.

Of his friends the most part were Cartesians ; they propounded to him difficulties which, they maintained, could only be solved by the principles of their Master. Mr. de Spinosa freed them from a certain error to which the learned men were then committed by satisfying them by means of entirely different arguments. But I marvel at the spirit of man and the force of prejudices : these friends on returning home were nearly overwhelmed when they made it public that Mr. des Cartes was not the only philosopher who deserved to be followed. The majority of the clergy, prepossessed with the doctrines of this great genius, and jealous of the right, which they believe they have, of being infallible in their choice, cry out against a rumour which offends them, and they do not neglect anything known to them in order to stop it at its source. But whatever they did the evil grew in such wise that there nearly appeared a civil war in the Empire of Letters, which was only arrested when our philosopher was entreated to explain openly his views on Mr. des Cartes. Mr. de Spinosa, who only wanted peace, voluntarily devoted some hours of his leisure to this work, and he had it printed in the year [1663].* In this work he proved geometrically 5 the first two parts of the *Principles* of Mr. des Cartes, of which he gives an account in the preface, which is from the pen of one of his friends. But, whatever he might say to the credit of this celebrated author, the partisans of this great man, being accused of atheism, consequently did all they could to let the storm break on our philosopher.

This persecution, which lasted as long as he lived, so far from shaking him, strengthened him in the search after Truth.

He attributed most of the vices of men to errors of the understanding, and, fearing lest he himself should fall into such error, he buried himself still deeper in solitude, leaving the place where he was staying then in order to go to Voorburg, where he believed it would be more peaceful.

---

5 This book is entitled *Renatus Descartes's Principles of Philosophy*, first and second parts demonstrated geometrically by Mr. D. S.

* A and T: 1664.

The real men of learning who discovered it, so to say, as soon as they did not continue to see him, did not take long to find him again and to overwhelm him with their visits in the latter village as they had done in the former. As he was not indifferent to the sincere affection of well-meaning people, he yielded immediately when they urged him to leave the country for some city where they might see him with less difficulty. Accordingly, he settled in the Hague, which he preferred to Amsterdam, because the air there was more healthy, and he stayed there uninterruptedly for the rest of his life.

At first he was only visited by a small number of friends who made moderate use of him. But as this lovely place is never without travellers who try to see all that is worth seeing, the most intelligent among them, whatever their station, would have considered their journey wasted if they had not paid him a visit. And as the reality corresponded with his renown, there were no men of learning who did not write to him in order to be enlightened about their doubts, as is testified by the large number of letters which form part of the Book [6] which was printed after his death. But the many visits which he

---

[6] This book containing his last works, which was printed after his death, has for its title *B. D. S. Posthumous Works.*

received, the many replies which he had to write to the scholars who wrote to him from everywhere, and these wonderful books which are to-day all our delight, did not sufficiently occupy this great Genius. He devoted each day some hours to the preparation of lenses for microscopes and telescopes, in which he excelled so much that there is reason to believe that, if death had not prevented it, he would have discovered the most beautiful secrets of Optics.

He was so ardent in the search for Truth that, although his health was very poor and required rest, he nevertheless took so little rest that once he did not go outside his lodgings during three whole months ; so ardent, indeed, that he declined an open professorship in the University of Heidelberg from fear lest such a post should interfere with his purpose.

After having taken such pains with the improvement of his understanding, it ought not to surprise anybody if all that he brought to light is of an inimitable character. Before his time Holy Scripture was an inaccessible sanctuary. All who had discussed it had done so blindly. He alone spoke about it like a scholar, in his *Treatise* 7 *on Theology and Politics*, for it is

7 This book is translated into French, and has for its title *The Key of the Sanctuary.*

certain that nobody had ever mastered Jewish Antiquities as well as he did.

Although there is no wound more dangerous than that inflicted by slander, nor any less easy to bear, he was never heard to show any resentment against those who injured him. Although many have tried to defame this book by means of insults full of gall and bitterness, yet, instead of making use of the same weapons in order to crush them, he contented himself [8] with elucidating the passages to which they gave a wrong meaning, fearing lest their malice should confuse sincere souls. If this book excited a torrent of persecutors against him, it is not since to-day that the thoughts of great men have been misinterpreted, and that a great reputation has proved to be more dangerous than a bad one.

He had so little craving for the goods of fortune that when, after the death of Mr. de Witt, who had given him a pension of two hundred francs, his heirs, on being shown the signed promise of Spinosa's Maecenas, made some difficulty about continuing to give him the pension, he left the document in their hands with as much calm as if he had resources elsewhere. This disinterested manner made them

[8] The author made comments on this book which are to be found at the end of the translation of the same book.

reconsider the matter, and they granted to him with pleasure what they had intended to refuse him. It was on this grant that the greater part of his subsistence depended, as he had inherited from his Father only some involved business affairs ; or rather those Jews with whom this good man had transacted business, judging that his son was not in the mood to unravel their tricks, embarrassed him in such a way that he preferred to abandon everything to them rather than sacrifice his peace to an uncertain hope.

He had such a great propensity not to do anything for the sake of being regarded and admired by the people, that when dying he requested that his name should not be put on his *Ethics*, saying that such affectations were unworthy of a philosopher.

His renown was so widespread that they spoke about him in the higher circles. Prince Condê, who was at Utrecht at the beginning of the war of 1672, sent him a safe-conduct with a friendly letter inviting him to come to see him. Mr. de Spinosa had a mind too well cultivated, and he knew too well what was due to a person of such high rank, to ignore on this occasion his duty to His Highness ; but, as he never quitted his solitude except to return to it soon afterwards, a journey of several weeks' duration made him hesitate. At last after some delays his friends persuaded him to set out on the journey. As an order from the King had, in the meantime, summoned the Prince elsewhere, M. de Luxembourg received Spinosa in the Prince's absence, showed him a thousand devotions, and assured him of the good will of His Highness. The crowd of courtiers did not awe our philosopher. He had a courteousness which was more like that of the Court than that of a commercial city such as he was born in, and one may say of it that it had no vices or faults. Although this kind of life was utterly opposed to his principles and to his taste, he submitted to it with as much complacency as the courtiers themselves. The Prince, who wanted to see him, frequently sent word that he should wait for him. The inquisitive, who liked him and always found something new to like about him, were delighted that His Highness obliged him to wait for him. After some weeks the Prince sent word that he could not return to Utrecht. All the inquisitive among the French were vexed, for our philosopher at once took his departure from them in spite of the gratifying offers which M. de Luxembourg made him.

He had a quality which I esteem all the more because it is rare in a philosopher. He was extremely tidy, and whenever he went out there was something about his clothes which usually distinguishes a gentleman from a pedant. " It is not," he said, " such untidy and neglected appearance that makes us scholars, on the contrary," he continued, " such affectation of negligence is the mark of an inferior mind, in which wisdom is not to be found at all, and in which the sciences can only breed impurity and corruption."

Not only did riches not tempt him at all, but he also had no fear whatever of the consequences of poverty. His virtue raised him above all these things, and although he was not very much in the good graces of Fortune he never coaxed her, neither did he murmur against her. But if his fortune was moderate, his soul was the better provided with that which makes men great. Though in extreme need, he was liberal, lending of what little he had, through the largesse of his friends, with as much generosity as if he rolled in wealth. When he heard that somebody who owed him two hundred francs had gone bankrupt, he was so far from being upset thereby that he said laughingly, " I must reduce my daily fare in order to make up for this small loss. It is at such a price," he added, " that one buys fortitude." I do not mention this action as something brilliant ; but, since there is nothing in which genius shows itself more clearly than in such small things, I could not omit it without scruple.

As he did not enjoy good health at any time in the whole course of his life, he had learnt to suffer since his most tender youth ; therefore nobody ever had a better understanding of that branch of knowledge. He did not seek consolation except in himself, and if he was susceptible to any sorrow, it was to the sorrow of others. He used to say that " to believe that an evil is less grievous when we have it in common with many other people is a great mark of ignorance, and one must have very little good sense to include community of tribulations among the number of consolations." It was in this spirit that he shed tears when he saw his fellow-citizens rend to pieces one who was a father to them all,9 and, although he knew better than anybody what men are capable of, he could not but shudder at that cruel sight. On the one hand, he saw an act of parricide that had not its like, and extreme ingratitude ; on the other hand, he saw himself deprived of an illustrious Maecenas, and of the sole support that was left to him. This was more than enough to overwhelm an

9 M. de Witt.

ordinary soul, but a soul like his, accustomed to overcome inner troubles, was far from succumbing to it. As he was always master of himself, he soon got over this terrible incident ; and when one of his friends who scarcely ever left him expressed his surprise thereat, our philosopher replied, " Of what use would wisdom be to us if after falling into the passions of the people we had not the strength to raise ourselves again by our own efforts ? "

As he espoused no party he showed preference for none, he allowed to each the liberty of its prejudices, but he maintained that most of them were a hindrance to Truth ; that reason was futile if one neglected to make use of it, or if the use of it was forbidden when there was occasion to make a choice. " There," he said, " are the two greatest and commonest faults of men, indolence and presumption. Some wallow lazily in a profound ignorance which reduces them below the level of brutes : others raise themselves as tyrants over the spirit of the simple, giving them a world of false ideas or thoughts as if they were eternal oracles. This is the source of those absurd beliefs with which men are so infatuated ; this it is that divides them from one another and sets itself in direct opposition to nature's aim, which is, to make them

66

similar, like the children of the same mother. That is why," he said, " only those who have broken away from the maxims of their childhood can attain to the knowledge of Truth, for one must make extraordinary efforts in order to overcome the impressions of custom and in order to efface the false ideas with which the minds of men are filled before they are able to judge about things for themselves." To get out of this abyss was, in his opinion, as great a miracle as to get order out of chaos.

One ought not, therefore, to be astonished if he waged war against superstition all his life ; apart from the fact that he was impelled thereto by a natural bent, the teachings of his Father, who was a man of good sense, contributed a great deal towards it. This good man had taught him not to confuse superstition with genuine piety, and wishing to test his son, who was only ten years old as yet, he instructed him to go and collect some money which a certain old woman in Amsterdam owed him. When he entered her house and found her reading the Bible she motioned to him to wait until she finished her prayer ; when she had finished it, the child told her his errand, and this good old woman, after counting her money out to him, said, as she pointed to it on the table, " Here is what I owe your father. May you some day be as upright a man as he is ; he has never departed from the Law of Moses, and Heaven will only bless you in the measure in which you will imitate him." As she was concluding these remarks she picked up the money in order to put it into the child's bag, but, having observed that this woman had all the marks of false piety against which his Father had warned him, he wanted to count it after her in spite of all her resistance. He found that he had to ask for two ducats, which the pious widow had dropped into a drawer through a slit specially made on the top of the table, and so he was confirmed in his thought. Elated by his success in this adventure, and by the praise of his Father, he watched these sort of people with more care than before, and he made such fine fun of them that everybody was astonished.

The object of all his actions was Virtue, but as he did not imitate the Stoics and form a frightful picture of her, he was no enemy of innocent pleasures. It is true that pleasures of the spirit were his principal study, and that those of the body touched him little. But when he found himself at such kinds of diversions as one cannot honestly dispense with, he took it as something indifferent, and without disturbing the tranquillity of his soul, which he preferred to all things imaginable. But what I esteem most in him is that, although he was born and bred in the midst of a gross people who are the source of superstition, he had imbibed no bitterness whatever, and that he had purged his soul of those false maxims with which so many are infatuated.

He was entirely cured of those silly and ridiculous opinions which the Jews have of God. A man who knew the end of sound philosophy and who, according to the unanimous view of the ablest men of our age, has best put it into practice, such a man, I say, was far from imagining about God what the people imagine about Him.

But because he did not believe Moses or the Prophets, since, as he said, they accommodated themselves to the grossness of the people, is that a reason for condemning him ? I have read most of the philosophers, and I assert in good faith that there is nothing that gives such beautiful ideas of the Deity as do the writings of Mr. de Spinosa.

He said that the more we know God the more are we masters of our passions ; that it is in this knowledge that one finds perfect tranquillity of spirit and the true love of God that brings us salvation, which is Blessedness and Freedom.

These are the principal points which according to the teaching of our philosopher are dictated by reason concerning the true life and the supreme good of man. Compare them with the doctrines of the New Testament, and you will see that they are just the same. The Law of Jesus Christ leads us to the love of God and of our neighbour, which is precisely what reason inspires us to do, according to the opinion of Mr. de Spinosa. Whence it is easy to infer that the reason why St. Paul calls the Christian religion [10] a reasonable religion is because reason prescribes it and is its foundation.[11] That which is called a reasonable religion is, according to Origen, whatever is subject to the sovereignty of reason.[12] One may add that one of the ancient Fathers asserts that we ought to live and to act according to the rules of reason.

So the opinions which our philosopher followed are supported by the Fathers and by Scripture ; yet he is condemned, but apparently only by those whose interest obliges them to speak against reason, or who have never known it. I make

[10] Rom. xii. 1.
[11] Erasmus in his notes on this passage.
[12] Theophrastus [Theophylaktos].

this slight digression in order to arouse the simple to throw off the yoke of envious and false scholars who cannot tolerate the reputation of good people and falsely accuse them of holding opinions little in harmony with the Truth.

To return to Mr. de Spinosa, his conversations had such an air of geniality and his comparisons were so just that he made everybody fall in unconsciously with his views. He was persuasive although he did not affect polished or elegant diction. He made himself so intelligible, and his discourse was so full of good sense, that none listened to him without deriving satisfaction.

These fine talents attracted to him all reasonable people, and whatever time it may have been one always found him in an even and agreeable humour.

Of all those who frequented him there was not one who did not show him special friendliness ; but since there is nothing so deceitful as the heart of man, it appeared subsequently that most of these friendships were feigned, those who were most indebted to him having treated him in the most ungrateful manner that one can imagine, without any ground, real or apparent.

These false friends who adored him to all appearances slandered him behind his back either

71

in order to court favour with those in power, who do not like people of intellect, or in order to gain a reputation by cavilling at him. One day when he heard that one of his greatest admirers tried to stir up the people and the Magistrate against him, he replied without emotion, " It is not from to-day that Truth costs dear, but it will not be slander that will make me abandon her." I would much like to know whether one has ever seen greater fortitude, or a purer virtue, and whether anyone of his enemies has ever done anything approaching such moderation ?

But I see well that his misfortune resulted from his being too good and too enlightened. He revealed to everybody what people wanted to be kept secret ; he found *The Key of the Sanctuary* [13] where people had seen nothing but vain mysteries. That was the reason why, thoroughly good man though he was, he could not live in security.

Although our philosopher was not one of those austere people who look upon marriage as a hindrance to the activities of the mind, he nevertheless did not enter into its bonds, either because he feared the ill temper of a woman, or

[13] This is a book which the author wrote in Latin entitled *A Theologico-Political Treatise,* and which is translated in French under the title of *The Key of the Sanctuary.*

THE HOUSE (×) IN WHICH SPINOZA DIED

"C'est d'ici peut-être que Dieu a été vu de plus près."—Renan

because the love of philosophy took him up completely.

Besides the fact that he was not of a very robust constitution, his strenuous application helped to enfeeble him still more ; and though there is nothing that drains one's strength so much as night-vigils, his vigils had become almost constant through the ill effects of a slight, slow fever which he contracted during his arduous meditations, and contracted so badly that after lingering during the last years of his life he ended it in the middle of its course.

Thus he lived forty-five years or thereabouts, having been born in the year 1632, and died on the twenty [first] * of February, 1677.

Should one also want to know something about his bearing and about his appearance, he was of medium height rather than tall, his facial expression was very genial and held one unconsciously.

He had a great, penetrating mind and a very complacent disposition. He had a wit so well seasoned that the most gentle and the most severe found very peculiar charms in it.

His days were few, but one may say nevertheless that he lived much, for he had acquired all that is truly good, namely virtue, and had

* second.

nothing more to desire after the great reputation which he acquired through his profound knowledge. Sobriety, patience and [veracity] * were but his lesser virtues ; and he may be declared fortunate because he died at the summit of his glory, unstained by any blemish, and leaving to the world of sage scholars the regret of seeing themselves bereft of a luminary that was not less useful to them than the light of the sun. For although he did not have the good fortune to see the end of the late wars, when the States [General] are resuming the government of their Empire half lost either through the fortune of arms, or as the result of an unfortunate choice, still it is no small happiness to have escaped the storm which his enemies were preparing for him.

They made him odious to the people because he furnished the means of distinguishing hypocrisy from genuine piety, and of destroying superstition.

Our philosopher is therefore very fortunate, not only in the glory of his [life],† but in the circumstances of his death, which he faced with an intrepid eye, as we have learned from those who were present, as if it had been easy for him to sacrifice himself for the sake of his enemies, so that their memory should not be stained by

* vivacity. † virtue.

74

parricide. It is we that are left who are to be pitied : that is, all those whom his writings have improved, and to whom his presence was moreover of great assistance on the road to Truth.

But since he could not escape the lot of all that has life, let us strive to walk in his footsteps, or at least to revere him with admiration and with praise, if we cannot imitate him. This is what I counsel to steadfast souls : to follow his maxims and his lights in such a way as to have them always before their eyes to serve as a rule for their actions.

That which we love and revere in great men lives still and will live through all the ages. The greater part of those who have lived in obscurity and without glory will remain buried in darkness and in oblivion. BARUCH DE SPINOSA will live in the remembrance of true scholars and in their writings, which are the temple of Immortality.

END

III

ADDITIONS TO THE OLDEST BIO-GRAPHY OF SPINOZA IN THE PRINTED TEXTS OF 1719 & 1735

[TRANSLATIONS]

ADDITIONS TO THE OLDEST BIOGRAPHY OF SPINOZA IN THE PRINTED TEXTS OF 1719 AND 1735

[TRANSLATIONS]

§ 1. *Advertisement.**

THERE is perhaps nothing that gives Free-thinkers a more plausible pretext to abuse Religion than the way in which its Defenders treat them. On the one hand they treat their Objections with the utmost contempt, and on the other they show the most ardent zeal in urging the suppression of the Books which contain these objections that they find so contemptible.

It must be admitted that this Procedure does injury to the Cause which they defend. In fact, if they were sure of its soundness would they be afraid that it might succumb if they supported it with good reasons only? And if they were filled with that strong confidence, with which Truth inspires those who believe that they are fighting for it, would they have had recourse to mean advantages and to wrong

---

* Not in A or T, nor in the *Nouvelles Litteraires* edition of 1719; only in some copies of the Le Vier edition of 1719, and not in the 1735 edition.

means in order to make it triumph ? Would they not rely solely on its power ; and, confident of victory, would they not voluntarily go to combat against Error armed like their opponents ? Would they feel uneasy about granting to the whole World the freedom to compare the reasons of both parties and to judge, in the light of such comparison, which side has the advantage ? Does not the withholding of this freedom encourage unbelievers to imagine that one dreads their Arguments, and that one finds it easier to suppress them than to expose their falsity ?

But although one is persuaded that the Publication of their strongest writings against the Truth, so far from doing it injury, will, on the contrary, only serve to make its Triumph more striking and their Defeat more humiliating, one nevertheless ventures against the current by publishing the Life and Spirit of Mr. Benedict de Spinosa.

Such few Copies of it have been printed that the book will scarcely be less rare than if it had remained in manuscript. Care will be taken to distribute the small number of Copies among competent People able to refute it. No doubt they will beat off the Author of this Treatise, and they will overthrow from top to bottom the impious System of Spinosa, on which the

Sophistries of his Disciple are based. This is the aim one set before himself in getting printed the Treatise from which the Free-thinkers draw their captious arguments.

It is given without any abridgement or mitigation, so that these People should not say that the difficulties have been reduced in order that the Refutation may be more easy. For the rest, the gross Insults, the Lies, the Calumnies, the Blasphemies, which one reads therein with horror and execration, already refute themselves and can only lead to his confusion who has expressed them with as much extravagance as impiety.

§ 2. *Preface of the Copyist.*[*]

BARUCH OR BENEDICT DE SPINOSA has acquired a name so little reputable in the World on account of his Doctrine and the singularity of his opinions about Religion, that, as the author of his *Life* says at the beginning of this Work, when one wants to write about him or in his favour, one has to hide himself with as much care and take as many precautions as if one were about to

---

[*] Not in A or T, but, with slight changes, it is in the *Nouvelles Litteraires* edition of 1719, with the editorial remark: " This Piece was sent to me with the Preface : I give it as I received it." In the 1735 edition it is given, with some omissions and additions, under the heading *Advertisement.*

commit a crime. However, we do not think we need make a Mystery about avowing that we have copied this Work from the Original, *the first part of which treats of the life of this Personage, and the second gives an idea of his Spirit.

The Author is forsooth unknown, although it is apparent that he who has composed it had been one of his Disciples, as he explains very clearly ! If, however, it were permitted to build something on conjectures, one might say, and maybe with certainty, that the whole Work was the doing of the late Mr. Lucas, so famous† for his *Quintessences*, but even more so for his morals and his mode of life.

Be that as it may, the Work is so rare as to deserve examination by Intellectual People. And it is only with a view to this that one has taken the trouble to make a ‡ copy of it. That is the whole aim we have set ourselves, leaving to others the task of making such reflections as they may judge appropriate.§

* The 1735 edition omits the rest of this sentence.
† The *Nouvelles Litteraires* edition inserts here " in these provinces."
‡ *Nouvelles Litteraires* edition has " this."
§ Instead of this whole paragraph the 1735 edition has the following statement :
" Most of the *Notes,* and the *Catalogue of the Writings of Spinosa,* have been added to this *new edition* by another of

§ 3. *Concerning the French Translation of the Tractatus Theologico-Politicus.*

Instead of Note 7 on page 60, the Le Vier edition of 1719, and the *Nouvelles Litteraires* edition of the same year, give fuller, though contradictory, accounts, as follows :

I. Le Vier : " It is entitled *Tractatus Theologico-Politicus,* etc. Hamburg, 1670. 4°. This book has been translated into French and published with three different Titles :

1. *Curious Reflections by a disinterested Mind on matters which are most important for both public and individual salvation.* Cologne, 1678. 12°.

2. *The Key of the Sanctuary.*

3. *Treatise on the Superstitious Ceremonies of the Jews both Ancient and Modern.* Amsterdam, 1678. 12°.

" These three titles do not show that three editions were issued of this Book. As a matter of fact there was only one edition ; but the

his Disciples." This is also stated already on the title-page of the 1735 edition, which reads as follows :

" The Life of Spinosa by one of his Disciples : unabridged new edition, augmented by some Notes and a Catalogue of his Writings by another of his Disciples, etc."

publisher had these different titles printed in turn in order to elude the inquisitors. With regard to the author of the French Translation, opinions are divided. Some attribute it to the late Mr. de St. Glain, Editor of the *Gazette of Rotterdam* [Amsterdam].

"Others claim it for Mr. Lucas, who has made himself famous by his *Quintessences*, which were always full of novel invectives against Louis XIV. What is certain is that the latter was a friend and disciple of Mr. de Spinosa, and that he is the author of this *Life* and of the Work which follows it."

II. Nouvelles Litteraires : "The Latin Title is *Tractatus Theologico-Politicus*. This book was translated into French by Mr. de S. Glain, an Angevin, Captain in the service of the States General, and who subsequently conducted the *Gazette of Rotterdam*. He had been a Calvinist, but after getting to know Spinosa he became one of his disciples and one of his greatest admirers. He called his Translation *The Key of the Sanctuary* ; but as this title roused a great deal of protest, especially in Catholic countries, it was thought advisable, in order to help the sale of it, to change its title, in the second edition, to that of a *Treatise on the Superstitious Ceremonies of the Jews both Ancient and Modern* ; and for the same reason, when a third edition appeared, it received the title of *Curious Reflections of a disinterested Mind.*"

§ 4. *Concerning S. J. de Vries.*

The following account (based on Colerus) is inserted in the Le Vier edition (but not in the *Nouvelles Litteraires* edition) after the first paragraph on page 65.

" He was as unselfish as the devotees, who cry out against him most, are little wont to be. We have already seen one * proof of his unselfishness, we will now relate another, which does him no less honour.

" When one of his intimate friends,† a well-to-do man, wanted to make him a present of two thousand Florins, so as to enable him to live more comfortably, he declined them with his usual politeness, saying that he had no need of them. As a matter of fact he was so temperate and so abstemious ‡ that he missed nothing, although he had very little. *Nature*, he used to say, *is content with little, and when she is satisfied, so am I.*

" But he was no less just than he was unselfish, as will be seen presently.

" The same friend who wanted to give him

---

* See above, p. 61 f. † Mr. Simon de Vries.

‡ On an average he did not expend as much as six sous a day, and he only drank one pint of wine in a month.

two thousand Florins, having neither wife nor children, formed the design of making a Will in his favour, and to appoint him his sole legatee. He spoke to him about it and wanted to persuade him to agree to it, but so far from agreeing to it, Mr. de Spinosa showed him so vividly that he would be acting unjustly and unnaturally if, to the cost of his own brother, he disposed of his estate in favour of a stranger, be his affection for him never so great, that his friend, yielding to his wise remonstrance, left all his fortune to him * who ought naturally to have been his heir, on condition, however, that he should pay to our philosopher a life-annuity of five hundred Florins. But again admire his unselfishness and his moderation, he considered this pension too large and had it reduced to three hundred Florins. A fine example, but little followed, especially by ecclesiastics, people who look with greed upon the possessions of another, who, taking advantage of the weakness of the old and of the devotees who are infatuated with them, not only unscrupulously accept legacies at the expense of natural heirs, but even resort to suggestion in order to procure them.

" But let us leave these hypocrites and return to our philosopher."

* To his brother.

§ 5. *Catalogue of the Works of Mr. de Spinosa.**

The Principles of Philosophy of René Descartes, demonstrated according to the geometrical method by Benedict de Spinosa, of Amsterdam. To which are added *Metaphysical Thoughts*, etc. Amsterdam, John Riewerts, 1663. 4°.

Theological and Political Treatise, etc. Hamburg, Henry Kunrath, 1670. 4°. This treatise has been reprinted with the title *The Collected Historical Works of Daniel Heinsius*, first part. Second edition, etc. Leyden, by Isaac Hercules, 1673. 8°. This edition is more correct than the quarto edition, which is the first.

B. D. S. *Posthumous Works*, 1677. 4°.

Apology of Benedict de Spinosa, in which he justifies his exit from the Synagogue. This Apology is written in Spanish, and has never been printed.

Treatise on the Iris or on the Rainbow, which he threw into the fire.

The Pentateuch, translated into Dutch, which he also threw into the fire.

Besides the above works, of which Mr. de Spinosa really is the author, the following have been attributed to him :

* Only in the Le Vier edition of 1719 and 1735.

Lucius Antistius Constans, *On Ecclesiastical Law*, a Singular Book, etc. Alethopolis, by Caius Valerius Pennatus, 1665. 8°. Mr. de Spinosa has assured his best friends that he was not the author of this book. It has been attributed to Mr. Louis Meyer, doctor in Amsterdam, to Mr. Herman Schelius, and to Mr. Van den Hooft, who showed his zeal in the United Provinces against the office of Stadtholder. According to all appearances it was the last who was its author, and he wrote it in order to avenge himself on the Dutch Clergy, who were strong partisans of the House of Orange, and who constantly declaimed from the Pulpit against Mr. Pensionary de Witt.

Philosophy the Interpreter of the Holy Scriptures, a Paradoxical Essay. Eleutheropolis, 1666. 4°. Public opinion attributes this work to Mr. Louis Meyer. This Treatise has been reprinted with the title of *The Collected Historical Works of Daniel Heinsius*, second part. Leyden, by Isaac Hercules, 1673. 8°.

All the works of Mr. de Spinosa, as well as those which are attributed to him, have been translated into Dutch by Mr. Jan Henry Glasmaker, the Perrot d'Ablancourt of Holland. Only the *Tractatus Theologico-Politicus* has been translated into French.   See page 60 of the *Life of Mr. de Spinosa.*

A Disciple of Mr. de Spinosa, named Abraham Jan Cuffeler, has written a Logic according to the Principles of his master.   It is entitled :

Specimen of Natural and Artificial Reasoning, serving as an introduction to the Principles of Pantosophy.   Hamburg, by Henry Kunrath, 1684.   8°.

[For other, minor additions see *Annotations* to pp. 56, 110-113.]

IV

LA VIE DE FEU
MONSIEUR DE SPINOSA

Si faute d'un pinceau fidelle
Du Fameux Spinosa l'on n'a pas peint les traits
La Sagesse etant immortelle
Ses Ecrits ne mourront jamais.*

* These rhymes are not in A, nor in the *Nouvelles Litteraires* edition of 1719, nor in the 1735 edition; but they are on the title-page of the Le Vier edition of 1719.

LA VIE DE FEU MONSIEUR DE SPINOSA

Notre siecle est fort eclairé, mais il n'en est pas
plus equitable à l'egard des grands Hommes.
Quoiqu'il leur doive ses plus belles lumieres, et
qu'il en profite heureusement, il ne peut souffrir
qu'on en * loue, soit par envie, ou par ignorance ;
et il est surprenant qu'il se faille cacher pour
ecrire leur vie, comme on fait, pour commettre
un crime ; particulierement si ces grands
Hommes sesont rendus celebres par des voies
extraordinaires, et inconnues aux ames communes. Car alors sous pretexte de faire honneur
aux opinions receues, quoiqu' absurdes et ridicules, ils defendent leur ignorance, à quoy ils
sacrifient les plus saines lumieres de la raison,
et, pour ainsi dire, la verité meme. Mais quelque
risque que l'on courre dans une carriere si epi-
neuse, j'aurois bien peu profité de la Philosophie
de celuy † dont j'entreprens d'ecrire la vie, et
les maximes, si je craignois de m'y engager.
Je crains peu la furie du peuple, aiant l'honneur
de vivre dans une Republique qui laisse à ses
Sujets la liberté des sentimens, et ou les souhaits
meme seroient inutiles pour etre heureux, si

* A : les.   † A : ce grand homme.

les personnes d'une probité eprouvée y etoient veües sans jalousie. Que si cet ouvrage, que je consacre à la memoire d'un illustre amy, n'est pas approuvé de tout le monde, il le sera pour le moins de ceux qui n'aiment que la Verité, et qui ont quelque sorte d'aversion· pour le vulgaire impertinent.

BARUCH DE SPINOSA etoit d'Amsterdam la plus belle ville de l'Europe, et d'une naissance fort mediocre : car son Pere qui etoit Juif et Portugais,* n'aiant pas le moien de la pousser dans le commerce, resolut de luy faire apprendre les lettres Hebraïques. Cette sorte d'etude qui est toute la science des Juifs, n'etoit pas capable de remplir un esprit brillant comme le sien. Il n'avoit pas quinze ans qu'il formoit des difficultés que les plus doctes d'entre les Juifs avoient de la peine à resoudre. Et quoiqu'une jeunesse si grande ne soit guerre † l'age de discernement, il en avoit assés pour s'apercevoir que ses doutes embarassoient le Maitre. De peur de l'irriter, il feignoit d'etre fort satisfait de ses reponses, se contentant de les ecrire pour s'en servir en temps et lieu. Comme il ne lisoit que la Bible, il se rendit bien tot capable de n'avoir plus besoin d'interprete ; il y faisoit des reflexions si justes que les Rabins ne repondoient qu'a la maniere

* T : Juif de nation et Portugais.   † A : n'etoit guéres.

des ignorans, qui voiant leur raison à bout, imposent a ceux qui les pressent trop, d'avoir des opinions peu conformes à la Religion. Un si bizarre procedé luy fit comprendre qu'il etoit inutile de s'informer de la Verité. " Le peuple " ne la connoit point ; d'ailleurs en croire " aveuglement les livres les plus authentiques, " c'est, disoit il, trop aimer les vieilles erreurs." * Il se resolut donc de n'en consulter plus † que luy meme, mais de n'epargner aucun soin pour en faire la decouverte. Il falloit avoir un esprit grand et d'une force extraordinaire pour concevoir au dessous de vingt ans un dessein de cette importance. En effet il fit bien tost voir qu'il n'avoit rien entrepris temerairement : car commencant tout de nouveau à lire l'Ecriture il en perça l'obscurité en developant ‡ les mysteres, et se fit jour au travers des nuages, derriere les quels on luy avoit dit que la Verité etoit cachée.

Apres l'examen de la Bible, il lut et relut le Talmud avec la meme exactitude ; et comme il n'y avoit personne qui l'egalast dans l'intelligence de l'Hebreux, il n'y trouvoit rien de dificile, ni rien aussi qui le satisfist : mais il etoit si judicieux, qu'il laissa meurir § ses pensées avant que de les approuver.

* A omits quotation marks. † A : ne plus consulter.
‡ A : endevelopant. § Not in A.

Cependant Morteïra Homme celebre entre les Juifs, et le moins ignorant de tous les Rabins de son temps, admiroit la conduite et le genie de son disciple. Il ne pouvoit comprendre qu'un jeune homme fust si modeste avec tant de penetration. Pour le connoitre à fond il l'eprouva en toute maniere, et avoua depuis qu'il ne trouvoit rien a redire tant en ses moeurs, qu'en la beauté de son esprit. L'approbation de Morteïra augmentant la bonne opinion que l'on avoit de son Disciple, ne luy donnoit point de vanité. Tout jeune qu'il etoit, par une prudence avancée, il faisoit peu de fond sur l'amitié et sur les louanges des hommes. D'ailleurs l'amour de la * Verité etoit si fort sa passion dominante qu'il ne voioit presque personne. Mais quelque precaution qu'il prist, il y a des rencontres ou l'on ne peut honnestement les eviter, quoiqu'elles soient souvent dangereuses.

Entre les plus ardens à lier commerce avec luy, deux jeunes hommes qui se disoient ses plus particuliers amis le conjurerent de leur dire ses veritables sentimens. Ils luy representerent que quels qu'ils fussent il n'avoit rien à craindre de leur part, leur curiosité n'ayant pour but que de s'eclaircir de leurs doutes. Le jeune Disciple etonné d'un discours si peu attendu, fut quelque temps sans leur repondre ; mais se voyant

* Not in A.

La Vie de feu

Monsieur de

Spinosa

Notre siecle est fort éclairé,
mais il n'en est pas plus equitable à
l'egard des grands Hommes. Quoiqu'
il leur doive ses plus belles lumieres, et
qu'il en profite heureusement, il ne peut
souffrir qu'on en loue, soit par envie, ou
par ignorance; et il est surprenant qu'
il se faille cacher pour écrire leur vie,
comme on fait, pour commettre un
crime; particulierement si ces grands
Hommes se sont rendus celebres par
des voies extraordinaires, et inconnuës

.A.

pressé il leur dit en riant, " Qu'ils avoient Moïse
" et les Prophetes qui etoient vrais Israelites,
" et qu'ils avoient decidé de tout, qu'ils les
" suivissent sans scrupule s'ils etoient * veritable-
" ment Israelites. A les en croire, rapartit un de
" ces jeunes hommes, je ne vois pas qu'il y ait
" d'Etre immateriel,† que Dieu n'ait point de
" corps, ni que l'ame soit immortele, ni que les
" Anges soient une substance reelle. Que vous
" en semble, continua-t-il, en s'addressant à
" notre Disciple ? Dieu a-t-il un corps ? Y
" a-t-il des Anges ? L'Ame est elle immortelle ?
" J'avoue, dit le Disciple, que ne trouvant rien
" d'immateriel ou ‡ d'incorporel dans la Bible,
" il n'y a nul inconvenient de croire que Dieu
" soit un corps,§ et ‖ ce ‖ d'autant plus que
" Dieu[1] etant grand, ainsi que parle le Prophete,
" il est impossible de comprendre une grandeur
" sans etendue, et par consequent qui ne soit
" un corps. Pour les Esprits il est certain que
" l'Ecriture ne dit point que ce soient des sub-
" stances reelles et permanentes, mais des ¶
" simples Phantômes nommés Anges, parce que
" Dieu s'en sert pour declarer sa volonté ; de

[1] Pseaume xlviii. 1.
* A : etoit.   † A : d'Etres immateriels.
‡ A : ny.   § A : corps créé.
‖ Not in A.   ¶ A : de.

" telle sorte que les Anges, et toute autre sorte
" d'Esprits, ne sont invisibles qu'a raison de leur
" mattiere tres subtile et Diaphane, qui ne peut
" etre vue que comme on voit les Phantomes
" dans un miroir, en songe ou dans la nuit ;
" de meme que Jacob vit dans une echelle en
" dormant des Anges monter et descendre.
" C'est pourquoy nous ne lisons point que les
" Juifs aient excommunié les Saduceens pour
" n'avoir point cru d'Anges à cause * que le
" vieil † Testament ne dit rien de leur creation.
" Pour ce qui est de l'Ame, par tout ou l'Ecriture
" en parle, ce mot d'Ame se prend simplement
" pour exprimer la Vie, ou pour tout ce qui est
" vivant.   Il seroit inutile de chercher de quoy
" apuier ‡ son immortalité.   Pour le contraire,
" il y est visible en cent § endroits, et il n'est rien
" si aisé que de le prouver : mais ce n'est icy
" ni le lieu, ni le temps d'en parler.   Le ‖ peu que
" vous en dites, repliqua l'un de ¶ deux Amis,
" convaincroit les plus incredules, mais ce n'est
" pas assés pour satisfaire vos Amis, à qui il
" faut quelque chose de plus solide ; joint que
" la matiere est trop importante, pour n'etre
" qu'effleurée.   Nous ne vous en quittons à **

* A : accause.   † A : vieux.
‡ A : appuyer.   § A : cents.
‖ A : la.   ¶ A : des.   ** pour le.

" present qu'a condition de la reprendre une
" autre fois." *

Le Disciple qui ne cherchoit qu'a rompre la
conversation leur promit tout ce qu'ils voulurent,
mais dans la suite il evita toutes les occasions, ou
ils tachoient de la renouer ; et se resouvenant
que la curiosité de l'homme a rarement bonne
intention, il etudia la conduite de ses Amis, ou
il trouva tant à redire, qu'il rompit avec eux, et
ne voulut plus leur parler.

Ses Amis s'etant aperceus du dessein qu'il
avoit formé, se contentoient † d'en murmurer
entre eux pendant qu'ils crurent que c'etoit pour
les eprouver, mais se voiant hors d'esperance
de le ‡ pouvoir flechir, ils jurerent de s'en venger,
et pour § le faire plus sensiblement, ils com-
mencerent par le decrier dans l'esprit du peuple.
" Qu'ils ‖ d'abusoient de croire que ce jeune
" homme pust ¶ devenir un des pilliers de la
" Sinagogue ; qu'il y avoit plus d'apparence
" qu'il en seroit le Destructeur, n'aiant que haine
" et que mépris pour la Loy de Moïse, qu'ils
" l'avoient frequenté sur le temoignage de Mor-
" teira ** ; mais qu'aiant reconnu que c'etoit un

---

* A omits quotation marks.   † A : contentirent.
‡ T : les.   § A : plus.
‖ A : . . . peuple et dire qu'ils . . .
¶ dût.   ** A : Mortera.

" impie, et que le Rabbin s'abusoit d'en avoir une
" bonne idée, son abord leur faisoit horreur." *

Ce faux bruit semé a la sourdine, devint bien
tost public, et lors qu'ils virent le temps propre
à le pousser plus vivement, ils firent leur raport
aux Juges de la Sinagogue, qu'ils animerent en
sorte, qu'ils penserent le condamner sans l'avoir
entendu. L'ardeur du premier feu passée (les
Sacrés Ministres du Temple n'etant pas exempts
de colere) ils le firent sommer de comparoitre
devant eux. Luy qui sentoit que sa conscience
ne luy reprochoit rien, alla gaiement à la Sinagogue, ou ses Juges luy dirent d'un visage abbatu,
et en hommes rougés du zele de la maison de
Dieu. " Qu'apres les bonnes esperances qu'ils
" avoient conceues de sa pieté, ils avoient de la
" peine à croire le mauvais bruit qui couroit de
" luy, qu'ils † l'appelloient pour en savoir la
" verité, et que c'etoit dans l'amertume de leur
" coeur, qu'ils le citoient, pour rendre raison de
" sa foy ; qu'il etoit accusé de plus enorme de
" tous les crimes, qui est le mepris de la Loy ;
" qu'ils souhaittoient ardemment qu'il s'en pust
" laver, mais que s'il etoit convaincu, il n'y avoit
" point de suplice assés rude pour le punir." ‡
En suite l'aiant conjuré de leur dire s'il etoit

---

* A omits quotation marks. † A : et.
‡ A omits quotation marks.

coupable, comme ils virent qu'il le nioit ses faux amis qui etoient presens deposerent effrontem^t *
" l'avoir ouy † se mocquer des Juifs comme de
" Gens superstitieux, nés et elevés dans l'ignor-
" ance, qui ne sçavent ce que c'est que Dieu, et
" qui neanmoins ont l'audace de se dire son
" Peuple, au mepris des autres Nations. Que
" pour la Loy elle avoit eté instituée par un
" homme plus adroit qu'eux à la verité en matiere
" de politique, mais qu'il ‡ n'etoit guerre § plus
" eclairé dans la Phisique, ni meme dans la
" Theologie ; qu'avec une once de bon sens
" on en decouvroit l'imposture, et qu'il falloit
" etre aussi stupide que les Hebreux du temps
" de Moïse, pour s'en raporter à ce galand
" homme." ‖

Cela joint par ses Libertins a ce qu'il avoit dit de Dieu, des Anges, et de l'Ame, ebranla les esprits, et luy fit crier Anatheme avant meme que l'Accusé eust le temps de s'en ¶ justifier.

Les Juges poussés d'un saint zele à venger leur Loy profanée, interrogent, pressent, intimident ; A quoy l'Accusé repondit, " Que ses grimaces " luy faissoient pitié, qu'il avoueroit ce qu'ils " disoient sur la deposition de si bons temoins,

---

* A : effrontemment.
‡ A : qui.
‖ A omits quotation marks.

† A : oüis.
§ A : guéres.
¶ A : se.

" s'il ne falloit pour le soustenir que des raisons
" incontestables." *

Cependant Morteira etant averty du peril ou
etoit son Disciple, court a grands pas à la Sinagogue, ou aiant pris place aupres des Juges,† il
luy demanda, " S'il se souvenoit du bon exemple
" qu'il luy avoit donné ?   Si sa revolte est‡ le
" fruit § du soin qu'il avoit pris de son education ?
" Et s'il ne craignoit point de tomber entre les
" mains du Dieu vivant ?   Que le Scandale etoit
" deja grand, mais qu'il etoit encore temps de se
" repentir." ‖

Apres que Morteira eut epuisé sa rhetorique,
sans pouvoir ¶ ebranler la fermeté de son Disciple,
d'un ton ** plus redoutable et en Chef de la Sinagogue, il le pressa de se determiner à la repentance,
ou à la peine, et protesta de l'excommunier, s'il
ne leur donnoit à l'instant des marques de resipis-
cence.   Le Disciple sans s'etonner luy repartit ;
" Qu'il connoissoit le poids de ses menaces, et
" qu'en revanche de la peine qu'il avoit prise à luy
" apprendre la langue Hebraïque, il vouloit bien
" luy enseigner la maniere d'excommunier." ††

A ces paroles le Rabin en colere vomit tout

---

* A omits quotation marks.   † A: du juge.
‡ A: etoit.   § A: prix.
‖ A omits quotation marks.   ¶ Not in A.
** A: d'autant.   †† A omits quotation marks.

son fiel contre luy, et apres quelques froids reproches romp l'assemblée, sort de la Sinagogue, et jure de n'y revenir que la foudre à la main ; mais quelque serment qu'il en fit, il ne croioit pas que son Disciple eust le courage de l'attendre. Il se trompa dans ses conjectures, car la suite fit voir que s'il etoit bien informé de la beauté de son esprit, il ne l'etoit pas de sa force. Le temps qu'on prit depuis pour luy representer en quel abisme il s'alloit jetter,* s'etant passé inutilement, on prit jour pour l'excommunier. Aussi tost qu'il l'apprit, il se disposa à la retraitte, et bien loin de s'en effraier, " A la bonne heure, " dit il à celuy qui luy † en apporta la nouvelle ; " on ne me force à rien que je n'eusse fait de moy " meme si je n'avois craint le Scandale ; mais " puis qu'on le veut de la sorte, j'entre avec joie " dans le chemin qui m'est ouvert, avec cette " consolation, que ma sortie sera plus innocente " que ne fut celle des premiers Hebreux de ‡ " l'Egypte ; quoique ma subsistance ne soit pas " mieux fondée que la leur, je ² n'emporte rien " a personne, et je me puis vanter quelque

---

² Il est dit dans l'Exode xii. 35, 36, que les Hebreux em- m-porterent aux Egyptiens de l'argent et des habits, qu'ils avoient empruntés par l'ordre de Moïse. [This is not in A.]

* A : il alloit se jetter.   † Not in A.

‡ A : hors de.

" injustice qu'on me fasse, qu'on n'a rien à me
" reprocher." *

Le peu d'habitude qu'il avoit depuis quelque
temps avec les Juifs, l'obligeant d'en faire avec
les Chretiens, il avoit lié amitié avec des personnes
d'esprit, qui luy disoient que c'etoit dommage
qu'il ne sçéust ni grec ni latin. Quelque versé
qu'il fust dans l'Hebreux, dans l'Italien, et dans
l'Espagnol, sans parler de l'Allemand, du Fla-
mend, et du Portugais, qui etoient ses langues
naturelles, il comprenoit assés de luy meme de
quelle importance il etoit d'en trouver le moien,
n'aiant point de bien de naissance ni d'amis de
force à le pousser.

Comme il y pensoit incessamment, et qu'il en
parloit dans toutes les rencontres, Van den Enden†
qui enseignoit avec succés le Grec et le Latin,
luy offrit ses soins et sa maison sans exiger
d'autre reconnoissance que le luy aider quelque
temps à instruire ses Ecoliers quand il en seroit
devenu capable.

Cependant Morteira irrité du mepris que son
Disciple faisoit de luy et de sa Loy, changea son
amitié en haine, et gousta en le foudroiant le
plaisir que les ames basses trouvent dans la
vengeance.

* A omits quotation marks.

† T : Hebden. A : . . . en toute rencontre. Van . . .

L'Excommunication des Juifs n'a rien de fort particulier ; cependant po^r ne rien obmettre de ce qui peut instruire le Lecteur, j'en toucheray icy les principales circonstances. Le Peuple etant assemblé dans la Sinagogue cette ceremonie qu'ils appellent Herim 3 se commence par allumer quantité de bougies noires, et par ouvrir le Tabernacle ou sont gardés les Livres * de la Loy. Apres le Chantre dans un lieu un† peu† elevé entonne d'une voix lugubre les paroles d'execration, pendant qu'un autre Chantre embouche un cor 4, et qu'on renverse les bougies pour les faire tomber goutte à goutte dans une cuve pleine de sang, à quoy le peuple animé d'une sainte horreur à la veue de ce noir spectacle respond Amen, d'un ton furieux, et qui temoigne le bon office qu'ils croiroient rendre à Dieu, s'ils dechiroient l'Excommunié ; ce qu'ils feroient sans doute, s'ils le rencontroient en ce temps là, ou en sortant de la Sinagogue. Sur quoy il est à remarquer que le bruit du cor, les bougies renversées et la cuve pleine de sang sont des circonstances qui ne s'observent qu'en cas de blaspheme que hors

---

3 Herim en Hebreux signifie Separation. [A : *Herin,* and omits note.]

4 Cor ou cornet appellé en Hebreux Sophar [Shophar]. [Not in A.]

* A : Tables ; cela . . .   † Not in A.

cela on se contente de fulminer l'excommunica-tion comme il se pratiqua à l'egard de Monsieur Spinosa qui n'estoit point convaincu d'avoir blasphemé, mais d'avoir manqué de respect et pour Moïse et pour la Loy.

L'Excommunication est d'un tel poids parmy les Juifs que le meilleur des amis de l'excommunié n'oseroit luy rendre service, ni meme luy parler sans tomber dans la meme peine. Aussi ceux qui redoutent * la douceur de la solitude, et l'imperti-nence du peuple, aiment mieux essuyer toute autre peine que l'Anatheme.

Monsieur de Spinosa qui avoit trouvé un Asyle ou il se croioit à couvert des insultes des Juifs, ne pensoit plus qu'a s'avancer dans les sciences humaines, ou avec un genie aussi excel-lent que le sien il n'avoit garde qu'il ne fist en fort peu de temps un progrés tres considerable.

Cependant les Juifs tout † troublés d'avoir manqué leur coup, et qu'un ‡ qu'ils vouloient perdre fust hors de leur puissance, luy imposerent un crime dont ils n'avoient pu le convaincre. Je parle des Juifs en general, car je n'oserois dire que Morteira et ses Collegues, tant il est vray de dire que ceux qui vivent de l'Autel ne pardonnent jamais, etoient ses plus grands ennemis. S'etre soustrait à leur jurisdiction, et subsister sans leurs

* A : redoute.　　† A : touts.　　‡ A : que celuy.

secours, c'etoit deux crimes qui leur sembloient irremissibles. Morteira sur tout ne pouvoit gouter que son Disciple et luy demeurassent dans une meme ville, apres l'affront qu'il croioit * en avoir receu. Mais comment faire pour l'en chasser ? Il n'etoit pas chef de la ville comme il l'etoit de la Sinagogue. Cependant la malice est si puissante à l'ombre d'un faux zele, que ce Vieillard en vint à bout, et voicy comment il s'y prit. Il se fait † escorter par un Rabin de meme trempe, et va trouver les Magistrats ausquels il represente que s'il avoit excommunié Mr de Spinosa, ce n'etoit pas pour des raisons communes, mais pour des blasphemes execrables contre Moïse et contre Dieu. Il exagere l'imposture par toutes les raisons qu'une sainte haine suggere à un coeur irreconciliable, et demande po^r ‡ conclusion que l'Accusé soit banny d'Amsterdam. A voir les manieres du Rabin, et avec quel empressement il declamoit contre son Disciple, il etoit aisé de juger que c'etoit moins un pieux zele, qu'une secrete rage qui l'incitoit à se venger. Aussi les Juges qui s'en apperceurent cherchant à eluder leur plaintes, les renvoierent aux Ministres. Ceux cy les aiant examinées s'y § trouverent embarassés. De la façon que l'accusé

* A : qu'ils croit.	† A : fit.
‡ A : pour.	§ A : se . . . de la . . .

se justifioit,* ils n'y remarquoient rien d'impie. D'autre costé l'accusateur etoit Rabin, et le rang qu'il tenoit les † faisoit souvenir du leur. Tout bien consideré ils ne puvent ‡ absoudre un homme que leur semblable vouloit § perdre, sans outrager le Ministere, et cette raison bonne ou mauvaise leur fit donner leur conclusion en faveur du Rabin. De sorte que les Magistrats qui n'oserent ‖ pas les dedire pour des raisons qu'on peut aisément deviner, condamnerent l'Accusé à un exil de quelque mois.

Par ce moien le Rabinisme fut vengé, mais il est vray que c'etoit moins l'intention directe des Juges, que pour se delivrer des crieries importunes des plus facheux de tous les hommes. Au reste cet arrest bien loin de nuire a M^r de ¶ Spinosa seconda l'envie qu'il avoit de quitter Amsterdam.

Aiant apris des sciences humaines ce qu'un Philosophe en doit sçavoir, il pensoit à se degager de la foule d'une grande Ville lors qu'on le vint inquieter ; ainsi ce ne fut pas la persecution qui l'en chassa, mais l'amour de la solitude, ou il ne doutoit point qu'il ** trouvast la Vertié. Cette forte passion qui luy donnoit peu de relache, luy

* A : deffendoit.   † A : leur.
‡ A : pouvoient.   § A : vouloient.
‖ A : n'osoient.   ¶ Not in A.
** T : qu'il ne . . .

LA VIE DE SPINOSA

fit quitter sa Patrie avec joie pour un village nommé Rhinburg ou eloigné de tous les obstacles qu'il ne pouvoit vaincre que par la fuite, il s'addonna entierement à la Philosophie. Comme il y avoit peu d'auteurs qui fussent de son goust, il eut recours à ses propres meditations, etant resolu d'eprouver jusqu'ou elles pouvoient * s'etendre. En quoy il a donné une si haute idée de la grandeur de son esprit, qu'il y a asseurement peu de personnes qui aient penetré si avant que luy, dans les matieres qu'il a traittées.

Il fut deux ans dans cette retraitte, ou quelque precaution qu'il prist pour eviter tout commerce avec ses amis, ses plus intimes l'y alloient voir de temps en temps, et ne le quittoient qu'avec peine.

De ses amis la plus part etoient Cartesiens ; ils luy proposoient des difficultés qu'ils pretendoient ne se pouvoir resoudre que par les principes de leur Maitre. Mr de Spinosa les desabusa d'une erreur ou les sçav^s † etoient alors, en les satisfaisant par des raisons tout ‡ opposées. Mais j'admire l'esprit de l'homme et la force des § prejugés ; ces Amis retournés chés eux faillirent à se faire assommer en publiant que M^r des Cartes ‖ n'etoit pas le seul Philosophe qui meri-

* elle pouvoit. † A : scavants.
‡ A : toutes. § A : de ses.
‖ A : Descartes.

109

tast d'etre suivy. La plus part des Ministres preoccupés de la doctrine de ce grand Genie,* jaloux du droit qu'ils croient avoir d'etre infaillibles dans leur choix crient contre un bruit qui les offense, et n'oublient rien de ce qu'ils sçavent pour l'eteindre dans sa source : mais quoiqu'ils fissent le mal croissoit de la † sorte qu'on etoit sur le point de voir une guerre civile dans l'Empire des Lettres, lors qu'il fut arresté qu'on prieroit notre Philosophe de s'expliquer ouvertement à l'egard de Monsieur des Cartes.‡ Mᵣ de Spinosa qui ne demandoit que la Paix, donna volontiers à ce travail quelques heures de son loisir, et le fit imprimer l'an [1663].§ Dans cet ouvrage il prouva geometriquement,⁵ les deux premieres parties des principes de Mᵣ des Cartes ‖ de quoy il rend raison dans la preface par la plume d'un de ses amis. Mais quoiqu'il ait pû dire à l'avantage de ce celebre autheur, les partisans de ce grand homme etant accusés d'Atheïsme ont fait depuis tout ce qu'ils ont pu pour faire tomber la tempeste sur notre Philosophe.

Cette persecution qui dura autant qu'il vécut,

---

5 Ce Livre est intitulé, *Renati des Cartes principiorum Philosophiæ* pars 1ᵃ et 2ᵃ more geometrico a Dᵒ D. S. demonstrata. [Not in A.]

* A: homme.   † Not in A.   ‡ A: Descartes.
§ A and T: 1664.   ‖ A: Descartes.

bien loin de l'ebranler, le fortifia dans la recherche de la Verité.

Il imputoit la plus part des vices des hommes aux erreurs de l'entendement, et de peur d'y tomber, il s'enfonça plus avant dans la solitude, quittant le lieu où il etoit, pour aller a Voorburg, où il crut etre plus en repos.

Les vrais sçavans qui le trouvoient à dire sitost qu'ils ne le voioient plus ne mirent guerre à le deterrer et à * l'accabler de leurs visites dans ce dernier village, comme ils avoient fait dans le premier. Luy qui n'etoit pas insensible au sincere amour des gens de bien, ceda à l'instance qu'ils luy firent de quitter la campagne pour quelque ville, ou ils le pussent voir avec moins de difficulté. Il s'habitua donc à la Haie † qu'il prefera à Amsterdam à cause ‡ que l'air y est plus sain, et il y demeura constamment le reste de sa vie.

D'abord il n'y fut visité que d'un petit nombre d'amis, qui en usoient moderement. Mais cet aimable lieu n'etant jamais sans voyageurs, qui cherchent à voir ce qui merite d'etre veu §, les plus intelligens d'entre eux, de quelque qualité qu'ils fussent, auroient crû perdre leur voyage, s'ils ne luy avoient rendu ‖ visite. Et comme les

---

* Not in A.

‡ A : accause.   § A : vû.

† A : Haye.

‖ A : rendus.

effets respondoient à la renommée, il n'y a point eu de sçavans qui ne luy aient * ecrit pour etre eclaircis de leurs † doutes, temoin ce grand nombre de lettres qui font partie du Livre [6] qu'on a imprimé apres sa mort. Mais tant de visites qu'il recevoit, tant de reponses qu'il avoit à faire aux sçavans qui luy ecrivoient de toute part,‡ et ces ouvrages merveilleux qui font aujourd'huy toutes nos delices, n'occupoient pas suffisamment ce grand Genie. Il emploioit tous les jours quelques heures à preparer des verres pour des microscopes et des Telescopes, en quoy il excelloit de sorte, que si la mort ne l'eust prevenu, il est à croire qu'il eust decouvert les plus beaux secrets de l'Optique.

Il etoit si ardent à la recherche de la Verité, que bien qu'il eust une santé fort languissante, et qui avoit besoin de relache il en prenoit neanmoins si peu, qu'il a eté trois mois entiers sans sortir du logis, Jusques la qu'il a refusé de professer publiquem^t § dans l'Academie d'Heijdelberg, de peur que cet employ ne le troublast dans son dessein.

Apres avoir pris tant de peine à rectifier son

---

[6] Ce Livre contiens ses dernieres oeuvres qu'on a imprimées apres sa mort et a pour titre *B.D.S. Opera posthuma.* [Not in A.]

* A : ait.   † A : eclaircy de ses.
‡ A : toutes parts.   § A : publiquement.

entendement, il ne se * faut pas etonner, si tout ce qu'il a mis au jour est d'un caractere inimitable. Avant luy, la Ste Ecriture etoit un † Sanctuaire inaccessible. Tous ceux qui en avoient parlé,‡ l'avoient fait en Aveugles. Luy seul en parloit comme savant dans son Traitté 7 de Theologie et de Politique, car il est certain que jamais l'homme § n'a possedé si bien que luy les Antiquités Judaïques.

Quoiqu'il n'y ait point de blessure plus dangereuse que celle de la Medisance, nimoins facile à suporter ; on ne l'a jamais ouy temoigner de ressentiment contre ceux qui le dechiroient. Plusieurs aiant taché de decrier ce Livre par des injures pleins de fiel et d'amertume, au lieu de se servir des memes armes pour les detruire, il se contenta 8 d'en eclaircir les endroits aux quels ‖ ils donnoient un faux sens de peur que leur malice n'eblouît les ames sinceres. Que si ce livre luy a suscité un torrent de persecuteurs, ce n'est pas d'aujourd'huy que l'on a mal interpreté les pensées des grands Hommes, et que la

---

7 Ce livre est traduit en François, et a pour titre La Clef du Sanctuaire. [Not in A.]

8 L'auteur a fait des remarques sur ce livre qui se trouvent a la fin de la traduction du meme livre. [Not in A.]

* Not in A. † A : au. ‡ T : parté.
§ T : homme. ‖ T : à qui.

grande reputation est plus dangereuse que la mauvaise.

Il avoit si peu d'empressement pour les biens de la fortune, qu'apres la mort de Monsr de Witt qui luy donnoit une pension de deux cent francs, aiant montré le seing de son Maecene aux heritiers qui faissoient quelque dificulté de la luy continuer, il le leur mit entre les mains avec autant de tranquillité, que s'il eust eû du fond d'ailleurs. Cette maniere desinteressée, les faisant rentrer en eux memes, ils luy accorderent avec joie ce qu'ils venoient de luy refuser, et c'est sur quoy etoit fondé le meilleur de sa subsistance, n'aiant herité de son Pere que quelques * afaires embrouillées ; ou plutot ceux † des Juifs avec lesquels ce bon homme avoit fait commerce, jugeant que son Fils n'etoit pas d'humeur à demesler leurs fourbes, l'embarasserent en sorte, qu'il aima mieux leur abandonner tout que de sacrifier son repos à une esperance incertaine.

Il avoit un si grand penchant a ne rien faire pour etre regardé et admiré du Peuple, qu'il recommanda en mourant de ne mettre point son nom a sa Morale, disant que ces affectations etoient indignes d'un Philosophe.

Sa Renommée s'etant tellement repandue, que l'on ‡ en parloit dans les Cercles. Monsieur

---

* A : des. † A : celles. ‡ A : qu'on.

Le Prince de Condé qui etoit à Utrecht au commencement de la Guerre de 1672, luy envoya
un sauf-conduit avec une lettre obligeante, pour
l'inviter a l'aller voir. Monsieur de Spinosa
avoit l'esprit trop bien tourné et scavoit trop
ce qu'il devoit à une personne d'un si haut rang,
pour ignorer en cette rencontre ce qu'il devoit
a Son Altesse ; mais ne quittant jamais sa Solitude, que pour y rentrer bien tost apres, un voyage
de quelques semaines le tenoit en suspens.
Enfin apres quelques remises, ses Amis le deter-
minerent à se mettre en chemin, pendant quoy
un ordre du Roy aiant appellé Monsr le Prince
ailleurs, Monsieur de Luxembourg qui le receut
en son absence luy fit mille caresses, et l'asseura
de la bienveillance de son Altesse. Cette foule
de Courtisans n'etonna pas notre Philosophe, il
avoit une politesse plus aprochante de la Cour,
que d'une ville de commerce, à qui il devoit sa
naissance, et dont on peut dire qu'il n'avoit ni
les vices ni les defauts. Encore que ce genre de
vie fust entierement opposé à ses maximes, et
à son goust, il s'y assujettit avec autant de com-
plaisance que les Courtisans meme. Monsieur
Le Prince qui le vouloit voir, mandoit souvent
qu'il l'attendist. Les Curieux qui l'aimoient et
qui trouvoient toujours en luy des * nouveaux

* A : quelques.

sujets de l'aimer, etoient ravis que Son Altesse l'obligeast de l'attendre. Apres * quelques Semaines Monsieur le Prince aiant mandé qu'il ne pouvoit retourner à Utrecht, tous les curieux d'entre les François en eurent du chagrin, car notre Philosophe prit en meme temps congé d'eux malgré les offres obligeantes que luy fit Monsieur de Luxembourg.

Il avoit une qualité que j'estime d'autant plus, qu'elle est rare dans un Philosophe. Il etoit extremement propre et ne sortoit jamais qu'il ne parust en ses habits ce qui distingue d'ordinaire † un honneste homme d'un Pedant. " Ce " n'est pas, disoit il, cet air mal propre et negligé " qui nous rend sçavans, au contraire, poursuivoit " il, cette negligence affectée est la marque " d'une ame basse, ou la sagesse ne se trouve " point et ou les sciences ne peuvent engendrer " qu'impureté et corruption." ‡

Les Richesses ne le tentoient point, mais il ne craignoit point aussi les suites de la Pauvreté. Sa Vertu l'avoit mis au dessus de toutes ces choses, et quoiqu'il ne fust pas fort avant dans les bonnes graces de la Fortune, il ne la cajeola § jamais, ni ne murmura aussi contre elle. Mais si sa fortune fut des plus mediocres, son ame

---

* A : mais apres.　　　　† A : ordinairement.
‡ A omits quotation marks.　§ A : cajolla.

fut des mieux pourvûe * de ce qui fait les grands hommes. Il etoit liberal dans une extreme necessité, prestant de ce peu qu'il avoit des largesses de ses amis avec autant de generosité, que s'il eust † eté dans l'opulence. Aiant appris qu'un homme qui † luy † devoit deux cens francs avoit fait banqueroute ; bien loin d'en etre emeu, " il faut, dit il, en souriant, " retrancher de mon ordinaire, pour reparer cette " petite perte, c'est a ce prix, ajouta-t-il, que " s'achette la fermeté." ‡ Je ne raporte pas cette action comme quelque chos d'eclatant ; mais comme il n'y a rien en quoy le genie paroisse davantage, qu'en ces sortes de petites choses, je n'ay pu l'obmettre sans scrupule.

N'aiant point eu de santé parfaite pendant tout le cours de sa vie, il avoit appris à souffrir dés sa plus tendre jeunesse ; aussi jamais homme n'entendit mieux cette science. Il ne cherchoit de consolation que dans luy meme, et s'il etoit sensible à quelque douleur, c'etoit la douleur d'autruy. " Croire le mal moins rude quand il " nous est commun avec plusieurs autres per- " sonnes, c'est, disoit il, une grande marque " d'ignorance, et c'est avoir bien peu de bon " sens que de mettre les peines communes au

* A : plus grandes et des mieux pourvües.
† Not in A.   ‡ A omits quotation marks.

" nombre des consolations." * C'est dans cet esprit qu'il versa des larmes lors qu'il vit ses Concitoyens dechirer leur Pere 9 commun, et quoiqu'il sçeust mieux qu' homme du monde de quoy les hommes sont capables, il ne laissa pas de fremir a ce cruel Spectacle. D'un costé il voioit commettre un parricide sans exemple, et une ingratitude extreme, d'un autre il se voioit privé d'un illustre Maecene, et du seul appuy qui luy restoit. C'en etoit trop pour terrasser une ame commune, mais une ame comme la sienne accoutumée a vaincre les troubles interieurs, n'avoit garde de succomber. Comme il † se † possedoit toujours il se vit bien tot au dessus de ce redoutable accident ; de quoy s'etonnant un de ses amis qui ne le quittoit gueres, " Que nous serviroit la sagesse," repartit notre Philosophe, " si en tombant dans les " passions du peuple, nous n'avions pas la force " de nous relever de nous memes." ‡

Comme il n'epousoit aucun party, il ne donnoit le prix a pas un, il laissoit à chacun la liberté de ses prejugés, mais il soutenoit que la pluspart etoient un obstacle à la Verité. Que la Raison etoit inutile, si on negligeoit d'en user, ou ‖

---

9 Monsieur de Witt. [Not in A.]
* A omits quotation marks.   † Not in A.
‡ A omits quotation marks.   ‖ A : et.

qu'on en deffendist l'usage, ou il s'agissoit de choisir. "Voila, disoit il, les deux plus grands " et plus ordinaires defauts des hommes, la " Paresse et la Presomption. Les uns croupissent " lâchement dans une profonde ignorance qui " les met au dessous des Brutes : les autres " s'elevent en Tyrans sur l'esprit des simples, " en leur donnant pour Oracles Eternels un " monde de fausses idées,* ou * pensées. C'est " là * la source de ces creances absurdes dont " les hommes sont infatués ; ce qui les divise " les uns des autres, et qui * s'oppose directement " au but de la nature, qui est de les rendre " uniformes, comme enfans d'une meme mere. " C'est pourquoy, il disoit, qu'il n'y avoit " que ceux qui s'etoient degagés des maximes " de leur enfance, qui pussent connoitre la Verité, " qu'il faut se faire d'etranges efforts pour " surmonter les impressions de la coutume, et " pour effacer les fausses idées, dont l'esprit des " hommes se remplit, avant qu'ils soient capables " de juger des choses par eux memes. Sortir de " cet abŷme etoit, a son avis, un aussi grand " miracle que de debrouiller le Chaos." †

Il ne faut donc pas s'etonner si il fit la guerre toute sa vie à la superstition ; outre qu'il y etoit porté par une pente naturele, Les enseignemens

* Not in A.   † A omits quotation marks.

de son Pere qui etoit homme de bon sens y avoient beaucoup contribué. Ce bon homme luy aiant appris à ne la pas confondre avec la solide pieté ; et voulant eprouver son fils qui n'avoit encore que dix ans, luy donna ordre d'aller recevoir quelque argent que luy devoit une certaine vieille femme d'Amsterdam. Entrant chés elle et la * trouvant qui lisoit dans la Bible, elle luy fit signe d'attendre qu'elle eust achevé sa priere ; laqu'elle etant finie, l'Enfant luy fit sa commission, et cette bonne vieille luy aiant conté son argent, voila, dit elle, en le luy montrant sur la table, ce que je dois a votre Pere, puissiés vous etre un jour aussi honneste homme que luy ; il ne s'est jamais ecarté de la Loy de Moïse, et le Ciel ne vous benira qu'autant que vous l'imiterés. Achev^t † ces paroles elle prit l'argent pour le mettre dans le sac de l'Enfant, mais luy, qui se ressouvenoit que cette femme avoit toutes les marques ‡ de la fausse Pieté dont son Pere l'avoit averty, le voulut conter apres elle malgré toute sa resistance, et y trouvant à dire deux Ducatons que la pieuse Veuve avoit fait tomber dans un tiroir par une fente faite expres au dessus de la table, il fut confirmé dans sa pensée. Enflé du succés de cette avanture, et que son Pere luy eust applaudy,

* A : le.   † A : Achevant.
‡ A inserts here : de la veritable hipocrisie et.

il observoit ces sortes de gens avec plus de soin qu'auparavant, et en faisoit des railleries si fines que tout le monde en etoit surpris.

Dans toutes ses actions la Vertu etoit son objet, mais comme il ne s'en faisoit pas une peinture affreuse, a l'imitation des Stoïques, il n'etoit pas ennemy des plaisirs honnestes. Il est vray que ceux de l'esprit faisoient sa principale etude, et que ceux du corps le touchoient peu : Mais quand il se trouvoit à ces sortes de Divertissemens dont on ne peut honnestement se dispenser, il les * prenoit comme une chose indifferente, et sans troubler la tranquillité de son ame, qu'il preferoit à toutes les choses imaginables : Mais ce que j'estime le plus en luy, c'est qu'etant né et elevé au milieu d'un peuple grossier qui est la source de la superstition, il n'en ait point succé l'amertume et qu'il se soit purgé l'esprit de ces fausses maximes dont tant de monde est infatué.

Il etoit tout a fait guery de ces opinions fades et ridicules que les Juifs ont de Dieu. Un homme qui sçavoit le fin de la saine Philosophie, et qui du consentement des plus habiles de notre siecle la mettoit le mieux en pratique. Un tel homme, dis je, n'avoit garde de s'imaginer de Dieu ce que le Peuple s'en imagine.

* T : le.

Mais pour n'en croire ni Moïse ni les Prophetes, lors qu'ils s'accommodent, comme il dit, à la grossiereté du Peuple, est ce une raison pour [le] * condamner ? J'ay leu † la pluspart des Philosophes, et j'asseure de bonne foy qu'il n'y en a point qui donne de plus belles idées de la Divinité que les Ecrits de Mr de Spinosa.

" Il dit que plus nous connoissons Dieu, plus " nous sommes Maitres de nos passions ; que " c'est dans cette connoissance qu'on trouve le " parfait acquiescement de l'esprit, et le veritable " amour de Dieu en quoi consiste nôtre salut, " qui est la Beatitude et la Liberté." ‡

Ce sont là les principaux points que notre Philosophe enseigne etre dictés par la raison touchant la veritable vie, et le souverain bien de l'homme. Comparés les avec les dogmes du nouveau Testament, et vous verrés que c'est toute la meme chose. La Loy de Jesus Christ nous porte à l'amour de Dieu et du Prochain, ce qui est proprement ce que la raison nous inspire, au sentiment de Monsieur de Spinosa. D'ou il est aisé d'inferer que la raison pour quoy St. Paul appelle la religion Chretienne [10] une religion raisonable, c'est que la raison la prescrit, et qu'elle

[10] Rom. xii. 1. [Not in A.]
* les.   † A : lû.
‡ A omits quotation marks.

en est le fondement.[11] Ce qui s'appelle religion raisonable etant, au rapport d'Origene, tout ce qui est soumis à l'empire de la raison.[12] Joint qu'un des anciens Peres asseure que nous devons vivre et agir suivant les regles de la raison.

Voila les sentimens qu'a suivy nôtre Philosophe appuié des PP. * et de l'Ecriture ; cependant il est condamné mais c'est apparemment par ceux que l'interest engage à parler contre la raison, ou qui ne l'ont jamais connue. Je fais cette petite digression pour inciter les simples à secouer le jong des envieux, et des faux savans, qui ne pouvant soufrir la reputation des gens de bien, leur imposent faussement d'avoir des opinions peu conformes à la Verité.

Pour revenir a Monsieur de † Spinosa, il avoit dans ses entretiens un air si engageant, et des comparaisons si justes, qu'il faisoit tomber insensiblement tout le monde dans son opinion. Il etoit persuasif quoiqu'il n'affectast de parler ni poliment, ni elegamm[t] ‡.   Il se rendoit si intelligible et son discours etoit si remply de bon sens, que nul ne l'entendoit qui n'en demeurast satisfait.

Ces beaux talens attiroient chés luy toutes les

[11] Erasme dans ses notes sur ce passage. [Not in A.]
[12] Theophraste [really *Theophylaktos*.   Not in A.]
 * A: Peres.   † Not in A.   ‡ A: elegamment.

personnes raisonables, et en quelque temps que ce fust on le trouvoit toujours d'une humeur egale et agreable.

De tous ceux qui le frequentoient il n'y en avoit pas un qui ne luy temoignast une amitié particuliere ; mais comme il n'est rien de si caché que le coeur de l'homme, on a veu par la suite que la plupart de ces amitiés etoient feintes ; ceux qui luy etoient les plus redevables, l'aiant traitté sans aucun sujet ni apparent ni veritable de la plus ingrate maniere qui se puisse imaginer. Ces faux amis qui l'adoroient en apparence, le dechiroient sous main, soit pour faire leur cour aux Puissances qui n'aiment pas les gens d'esprit, soit pour s'acquerir de la reputation en le chicanant. Un jour aiant appris qu'un de ses plus grands admirateurs tachoit de soulever le Peuple et le Magistrat, il repondit sans emotion, " Ce n'est " pas d'aujourd'huy que la Verité coute cher, " ce ne sera pas la Medisance qui me la fera " abbandonner." * Je voudrois bien sçavoir si l'on a jamais veu plus de fermeté et une Vertu plus epurée, et si aucun de ses Ennemis a jamais rien fait qui approche d'une telle moderation ? †

Mais je vois bien que son malheur etoit d'etre trop bon, et trop eclairé. Il a decouvert à tout le monde ce qu'on vouloit tenir caché, il a trouvé

* A omits quotation marks.   † A : full stop.

la[13] Clef du Sanctuaire ou l'on ne voioit que de vains mysteres. Voila pourquoy tout homme de bien qu'il etoit il n'a pu vivre en seureté.

Encore que notre Philosophe ne fust pas de ces gens severes, qui considerent le Mariage comme un empechement aux exercices de l'esprit il ne s'y engagea pourtant pas, soit qu'il craignist la mauvaise humeur d'une femme, ou que l'amour de la Philosophie l'accupast tout entier.

Outre* qu'il n'etoit pas d'une complexion fort robuste, sa grande application aidoit encore à l'affoiblir ; et comme il n'y a rien qui desseiche tant que les veilles, les siennes etoient devenues presque continuelles par la malignité d'une petite fievre lente qu'il avoit contractée dans ses ardentes meditations : si bien qu'apres avoir languy les dernieres années de sa vie, il la finit au milieu de sa course.

Ainsi il a vescu quarante cinque ans ou environ, etant né l'an mil six cens trente deux, et mort le vingt [uniéme]† Fevrier mil six cent septante sept.

Que si l'on desire aussi savoir quelque chose de

13 C'est un livre que l'Auteur a fait en Latin intitulé *Tractatus Theologico-Politicus,* lequel est traduit en françois sous le titre de *La Clef du Sanctuaire.* [Not in A.]

* A : Encore.   † deuxieme.

son port et de sa façon ; il etoit de moienne taille plustost que grand, d'une mine assés agreable, et qui engageoit insensiblement.

Il avoit l'esprit grand, penetrant, et l'humeur fort complaisante. Il avoit une raillerie si bien assaisonnée que les plus delicats et les plus severes y trouvoient des charmes tout particuliers.

Ses jours ont eté courts, mais on peut dire neanmoins qu'il a beaucoup vescu, aiant acquis les veritables biens qui consistent dans la Vertu, et n'aiant plus rien à souhaitter apres la haute reputation qu'il s'est acquise par son profond savoir. La Sobrieté, la Patience, et la [veracité]* n'etoient que ses moindres vertus ; et il se peut dire hereux d'etre mort au plus haut point de sa gloire, sans l'avoir souillée d'aucune tache ; laissant au monde des sages sçavans le regret de se voir privé d'une lumiere qui ne leur etoit pas moins utile que la lumiere du soleil. Car quoiqu'il n'ait pas en le bien de voir la fin des dernieres gueres, ou Messieurs les Etats [Generaux] reprennent le gouvernement de leur Empire à demy perdu, soit par le sort des armes, ou par le sort d'un malheureux choix, ce n'est pas un petit bonheur d'avoir echappé à la tempeste que ses ennemis luy preparoient.

* vivacité.

Ils le rendirent odieux au Peuple parce qu'il donnoit les moiens de distinguer l'Hipochrisie de la veritable Pieté, et d'eteindre la Superstition.

Notre Philosophe est donc bien heureux, non seulement par la gloire de sa [vie]* mais par les circonstances de sa mort, qu'il a regardée d'un oeil intrepide, ainsi que nous l'avons appris de ceux qui etoient presens, comme s'il eust eté bien aise de se sacrifier pour ses ennemis, afin que leur memoire ne fust pas souillée de son parricide. C'est nous qui restons qui sommes à plaindre : ce sont tous ceux que ses ecrits ont rectifiés, et à qui sa presence etoit encore d'un grand secours dans le chemin de la verité.

Mais puisqu'il n'a pu eviter le sort de tout ce qui a vie, tachons de marcher sur ses traces, ou du moins de le † reverer par l'admiration et par la louange, si nous ne pouvons l'imiter. C'est ce que, je conseille aux ames solides, de suivre tellement ses maximes et ses lumieres, qu'elles les aient toujours devant les yeux pour servir de regle a leurs actions.

Ce que nous aimons et reverons dans les Grands hommes est toujours vivant et vivra dans tous les siecles. La plus part de ceux qui ont vescu dans l'obscurité et sans gloire demeureront

* vertu.   † T : les.

ensevelis dans les Tenebres et dans l'oubly. BARUCH DE SPINOSA vivra dans le souvenir des vrais sçavans et dans leurs ecrits qui sont le temple de l'Immortalité.

FIN

V

ADDITIONS TO THE OLDEST BIO-GRAPHY OF SPINOZA IN THE PRINTED TEXTS OF 1719 & 1735

[FRENCH TEXTS]

ADDITIONS TO THE OLDEST BIOGRAPHY OF
SPINOZA IN THE PRINTED TEXTS OF 1719
AND 1735

[FRENCH TEXTS]

§ 1. *Avertissement.**

IL n'y a peut-être rien, qui donne aux Esprits
forts un pretexte plus plausible d'insulter à la
Religion, que la manière, dont en agissent avec
eux ses Deffenseurs. D'une part ils traittent
leurs Objections avec le dernier mépris et de
l'autre ils sollicitent avec le Zéle le plus ardent
la suppression des Livres, qui contiennent ces
Objections, qu'ils trouvent si méprisables.

Il faut avoüer, que ce Procédé fait tort à la
Cause qu'ils deffendent. En effet, s'ils étoient
assûrez de sa bonté, craindroient-ils, qu'elle ne
succombât en ne la soûtenant que par de bonnes
raisons ? Et s'ils étoient pleins de cette ferme
confiance, qu'inspire la Vérité à ceux, qui croyent
combattre pour elle, auroient-ils recours à de
faux avantages et à de mauvaises voyes pour la
faire triompher ? Ne se reposeroient-ils pas

---

* Not in A or T, nor in the *Nouvelles Litteraires* edition of
La Vie de Spinosa (1719); only in some copies of the Le Vier
edition, and not in the 1735 edition.

uniquement sur sa force ; et sûrs de la Victoire ne s'exposeroient-ils pas volontiers au Combat à Armes égales contre l'Erreur ? Appréhendroient-ils de laisser à tout le Monde la liberté de comparer les raisons de part et d'autre et de juger par cette comparaison, de quel côté est l'avantage ? Ôter cette liberté, n'est ce pas donner lieu aux Incrédules de s'imaginer, qu'on redoute leurs Raisonnements et qu'on trouve, qu'il est plus aisé de les supprimer, que d'en faire voir la fausseté ?

Mais bien qu'on soit persuadé, que la Publication de ce qu'ils ecrivent de plus fort contre la Vérité, loin de lui nuire, ne serviroit au contraire qu'à rendre son Triomphe plus éclatant et leur Défaite plus honteuse, néanmoins on n'a osé aller contre le torrent, en rendant publique La vie et L'Esprit de Monsieur Benoit de Spinoza.

On en a tiré si peu d'Exemplaires, que l'ouvrage ne sera guères moins rares, que s'il étoit resté en Manuscrit. C'est aux habiles Gens, capables de le refuter, qu'on aura soin de distribuer ce petit nombre d'Exemplaires. On ne doute point, qu'ils ne ménent battant l'Autheur de cet Ecrit monstrueux et qu'ils ne renversent de fond a comble le Systême impie de Spinosa, sur lequel sont fondez les Sophismes de son Disciple. C'est le but, qu'on s'est proposé en faissant imprimer

132

ce Traité, où les Libertins vont puiser leurs arguments captieux.

On le donne sans aucun retranchement ni adoucissement, affin que ces Messieurs ne disent point qu'on en ait énervé les difficultez pour en rendre la Réfutation plus aisée. D'ailleurs les Injures grossiéres, les Mensonges, les Calomnies, les Blasphêmes, qu'on y lira avec horreur et exécration, se réfutent assez d'eux mêmes et ne peuvent tourner qu'à la confusion de celui, qui les a avancez avec autant d'extravagance que d'impiété.

§ 2. *Preface du Copiste.**

BARUCH ou BENOIT † DE SPINOSA s'est acquis un nom si peu honorable dans le Monde par rapport à sa Doctrine et à la singularité de ses Sentimens en fait de Religion, que, comme dit l'Autheur de sa Vie au commencement de cet Ouvrage, il faut se cacher, quand on veut écrire

---

* Not in A or T, only in some copies of the Le Vier edition of 1719; but it is also in the *Nouvelles Litteraires* edition, in which it is headed simply "Preface" with the additional remark: "Cette Pièce m'a été envoyée avec la Preface: je la donne telle que je l'aie reçuë." In the 1735 edition it is given, with some omissions and additions, under the heading *Avertissement.*

† *Nouvelles Litteraires*: Benedict.

de lui, ou en sa faveur, avec autant de soin, et user d'autant de précaution, que si l'on avoit un crime à commettre. Cependant, nous ne croyons pas devoir faire Mystère d'avoüer, que nous avons copié cet Ecrit d'après l'Original,* dont la premiere partie traite de la vie de ce Personnage, et la seconde fournit une idée de son Esprit.*

L'Autheur en est inconnu à la vérité, quoi qu'il y aît apparence, que celui qui l'a composé aît été un de ses Disciples, comme il s'en explique assez clairement. Cependant, s'il étoit permis sur des conjectures de poser quelque fondement, on pourroit dire, et peut-être avec certitude, que tout l'Ouvrage est du fait du feu Sieur Lucas, si fameux † par ses *Quintessences*, mais encore plus par ses moeurs et par sa manière de vivre.

Quoi qu'il en soit, l'Ouvrage est assez rare pour mériter d'être examiné par des Personnes d'Esprit. Et c'est dans cette seule vuë, qu'on a pris la peine d'en faire une ‡ Copie. Voilà tout le but que nous nous sommes proposé,

---

* All the words between the asterisks are omitted in the 1735 edition.

† The *Nouvelles Litteraires* edition adds here: " dans ces Provinces."

‡ *Nouvelles Litteraires* edition has *cette*.

laissant aux autres le soin d'y faire telles reflexions, qu'ils jugeront à propos.*

§ 3. *Concerning the French Translation of the Tractatus Theologico-Politicus.*

Instead of Note 7 on page 113 the Le Vier edition of 1719 and the *Nouvelles Litteraires* edition of the same year give fuller, though contradictory, accounts as follows :

I. LE VIER : " Il est intitulé *Tractatus Theologico-Politicus*, etc. Hamburgi 1670. 4°. Ce livre a été traduit en Francois et publié sous trois Titres différens.

1. Sous celui de *Réflexions curieuses d'un Esprit desintéressé sur les matiéres les plus importantes au salut, tant public que particulier. Cologne* 1678. *In* 12°.

2. Sous celui de *Clef du Sanctuaire.*

* Instead of this whole paragraph the 1735 edition has the following statement :

" La plupart des *Notes*, et de *Catalogue des Ecrits de Spinosa*, ont été ajoutez à cette *nouvelle Edition* par un autre de ses Disciples." This is already stated on the title-page of this edition, which reads :

" *La Vie de Spinosa* par un de ses Disciples : Nouvelle Edition non tronque'e, augmentée de quelque Notes et du Catalogue de ses Ecrits par un autre de ses Disciple etc."

3. Enfin sous celui de *Traité des Cérémonies superstitieuses des* Juifs *tant Anciens que Modernes. Amsterdam* 1678. 12°.

Ces trois titres ne prouvent pas que l'on aît fait trois Editions de ce Livre. En effet il n'y en a jamais eu qu'une ; mais le Libraire a fait imprimer successivement ces différens titres pour tromper les Inquisiteurs. A l'égard de l'Autheur de la Traduction Françoise les sentimens sont partagez. Les uns la donnent au feu Sr. de St. Glain, Autheur de la Gazette de Rotterdam.

D'autres prétendent que c'est le Sr. Lucas, qui s'est rendu célébre par des *Quintessences*, toujours remplies d'invectives nouvelles contre Louis XIV. Ce qu'il y a de certain c'est que ce dernier étoit Ami et Disciple de Mr. de Spinosa, et qu'il est Autheur de cette Vie et de l'Ouvrage qui la suit."

II. Nouvelles Litteraires : " Le Titre Latin est *Tractatus Theologico-Politicus.* Cet ouvrage à eté traduit en François par le Sieur de S. Glain, Angevin, Capitaine au service de Messrs. les Etats, et qui a ensuite travaillé à la *Gazette de Rotterdam.* Il avoit été Calviniste, mais dès qu'il eût connu Spinosa, il devint un de ses Disciples et de ses plus grands Admirateurs. Il intitula sa Traduction *la Clef du Sanctuaire* ;

mais ce Titre aiant fait beaucoup de bruit, sur tout dans les Pays Catholiques, pour en faciliter le debit on jugea à propos dans une seconde edition de la changer en celui de *Traité des Ceremonies Superstitieuses des Juifs tant Anciens que Modernes*; et pour la même raison, lorsqu'on en fit une troisiéme Edition, on l'intitula *Reflexions curieuses d'un Esprit desintéressé*."

§ 4. *Concerning S. J. de Vries.*

The following account (based on Colerus) is inserted in the Le Vier edition (but not in the *Nouvelles Litteraires* edition) after the first paragraph on page 117.

" Il étoit aussi desintéressé que les Dévots qui crient le plus contre lui le sont peu. Nous avons déja vû une (*a*) preuve de son desinteressement, nous allons en rapporter une autre, qui ne lui fera pas moins d'honneur.

Un de ses (*b*) Amis intimes, Homme aisé, lui voulant faire présent de deux mille Florins, pour le mettre en état de vivre plus commodément, il les refusa avec sa politesse ordinaire, disant qu'il n'en avoit pas besoin. En effet il étoit si tempérant et si (*c*) sobre, qu'avec très peu de bien il ne

(*a*) Voyez cy-dessus pag. 114.   (*b*) Mr. Simon de Vries.
(*c*) Il ne dépensoit pas six sols par jour l'un portant l'autre, et ne buvoit qu'une pinte de vin par Mois.

manquoit de rien. *La Nature,* disoit-il, *est contente de peu, et quand elle est satisfaite, je le suis aussi.*

Mais il n'étoit pas moins équitable que desintéressé, comme on le va voir.

Le même Ami, qui lui avoit voulu donner deux mille Florins, n'ayant ni Femme ni Enfens, avoit dessein de faire un Testament en sa faveur et de l'instituer son Légataire universel. Il lui en parla et voulut l'engager à y consentir, mais bien loin d'y donner les mains, Mr. de Spinosa lui représenta si vivement qu'il agiroit contre l'équité et contre la Nature, si au préjudice d'un propre Frère il disposoit de sa succession en faveur d'un Etranger, quelqu'amitié qu'il eût pour lui, que son Ami, se rendant à ses sages remontrances, laissa tout son bien à (*a*) celui qui en devoit naturellement être l'Héritier, à condition toutes fois, qu'il feroit une Pension viagére de cinq cens Florins à nôtre Philosophe. Mais admirez encore ici son desintéressement et sa modération, il trouva cette Pension trop forte et la fit réduire à trois cens Florins. Bel exemple qui sera peu suivi, surtout des Ecclésiastiques, Gens avides du bien d'autrui, qui abusant de la foiblesse des Vieillards et des Dévotes qu'ils infatuent, non seulement acceptent sans scruples

(*a*) A son Frère.

des Successions au préjudice des Héritiers legitimes ; mais même ont recours à la suggestion pour se les procurer.

Mais laissons là ces Tartuffes, et revenons à nôtre Philosophe."

§ 5. *Catalogue des Ouvrages de Mr. de Spinosa.**

Renati Descartes Principiorum Philosophiae, more geometrico demonstratae, per Benedictum de Spinosa Amstelodamensem. Accesserunt ejusdem Cogitata Metaphysica etc. Amst. apud Johan. Riewerts 1663. 4°.

Tractatus Theologico-Politicus etc. Hamburgi, apud Henricum Kunrath, 1670. 4°. Ce même Ouvrage a été réimprimé sous le Titre de Danielis Hensii P. P. *Operum Historicorum Collectio Prima.* Editio secunda etc. Lugd. Batav. apud Isaacum Herculis 1673. 8°. Cette Edition est plus correcte que l'in-Quarto, qui est prémiére.

B. D. S. *Opera posthuma*, 1677. 4°.

Apologie de Benoit de Spinosa, où il justifie sa sortie de la Synagogue. Cette Apologie est écrite en Espagnol, et n'a jamais été imprimée.

Traite de l'Iris ou de l'Arc-en-Ciel, qu'il a jetté au feu.

* Only in the Le Vier edition of 1719 and 1735.

Le Pentateuque, traduit en Hollandois, qu'il a aussi jetté au feu.

Outre les Ouvrages cy-dessus, dont Mr. de Spinosa est véritablement l'Autheur, on lui a attribué les suivans :

Lucii Antistii Constantis *De Jure Ecclesiasticorum*, Liber Singularis etc. Alethopoli, apud Caium Valerium Pennatum 1665. 8°. Mr. de Spinosa a assuré ses meilleurs Amis qu'il n'etoit point l'Autheur de ce Livre. On l'a attribué à Mr. Louis Meyer, Médecin d'Amsterdam, à Mr. Hermanus Schelius et à Mr. Van den Hooft, qui a signalé son zéle dans les Provinces-Unies, contre le Stat-houdérat. Toutes les apparences sont que c'est ce dernier qui en est l'Autheur, et qu'il l'a écrit pour se venger des Ministres de Hollande, qui étoient grands Partisans de la Maison d'Orange, et qui déclamoient perpétuellement en Chaire contre Mr. le Pensionnaire de Wit.

Philosophia Sacrae Scripturae Interpres, Exercitatio paradoxa, Eleutheropoli 1666. 4°. La voix publique donne cet Ouvrage à Mr. Louis Meyer. Ce Traité a été réimprimé sous le Titre de *Danielis Heinsii P. P. Operum Historicorum collectio secunda*. Lugd. Batav. apud Isaacum Herculis, 1673. 8°

Toutes les Oeuvres de Mr. de Spinosa, aussi

bien que celles qui lui sont attribuées, ont été traduites en Hollandois par Mr. Jean Hendrik Glasmaker, le Perrot d'Ablancourt de Hollande. Il n'y a que le *Tractatus Theologico-Politicus*, qui aît été traduit en François. Voyez pag. 113 de *La Vie de Mr. de Spinosa*.

Un Disciple de Mr. de Spinosa, nommé Abraham Jean Cuffeler, a fait une Logique dans les Principes de son Maître. Elle est intitulée :

Specimen Artis Ratiocinandi Naturalis et Artificialis ad Pantosophiae principia manuducens. Hamburgi, apud Henricum Kunrath, 1684. 8°.

[For other, minor additions, see *Annotations* to pp. 56, 110–113.]

VI

ADDITIONAL BIOGRAPHICAL MATTER

[1656—1702]

[TRANSLATIONS]

ADDITIONAL BIOGRAPHICAL MATTER

[1656–1702]

§1. *The Excommunication of Spinoza,*
5416 [1656].

RECORD of the Excommunication which was pronounced against Baruch Espinoza, on the 6th Ab [27th July], in front of the Ark [in the Synagogue].

The Wardens make it known to you that they have long since been cognisant of the wrong opinions and behaviour of Baruch de Espinoza, and tried various means and promises to dissuade him from his evil ways. But as they effected no improvement, obtaining on the contrary more information every day of the horrible heresies which he practised and taught, and of the monstrous actions which he performed, and as they had many trustworthy witnesses who in the presence of the same Espinoza reported and testified against him and convicted him ; and after all this had been investigated in the presence of the Rabbis, they decided with the consent of these that the same Espinoza should be excommunicated and separated from the people of

Israel, as they now excommunicate him with the following excommunication :

" After the judgment of the Angels, and with that of the Saints, we excommunicate, expel and curse and damn Baruch de Espinoza with the consent of God, Blessed be He, and with the consent of all the Holy Congregation, in front of the holy Scrolls [Scriptures] with the six-hundred-and-thirteen precepts which are written therein, with the excommunication with which Joshua banned Jericho, with the curse with which Elisha cursed the boys, and with all the curses which are written in the Law [Pentateuch]. Cursed be he by day and cursed be he by night ; cursed be he when he lies down, and cursed be he when he rises up ; cursed be he when he goes out, and cursed be he when he comes in. The Lord will not pardon him ; the anger and wrath of the Lord will rage against this man, and bring upon him all the curses which are written in the Book of the Law, and the Lord will destroy his name from under the Heavens, and the Lord will separate him to his injury from all the tribes of Israel with all the curses of the firmament, which are written in the Book of the Law. But you who cleave unto the Lord your God are all alive this day." We order that nobody should communicate with him orally or in writing, or show him

146

any favour, or stay with him under the same roof, or within four ells of him, or read anything composed or written by him.

[Written in Spanish. Text published in Van Vloten's *Supplementum* (or vol. iv of Bruder's edition of Spinoza's Works), p. 290.]

§ 2. *From Ludovicus Meyer's Preface to Spinoza's Geometric Version of Descartes's " Principia "* (1663).

" . . . It pleased me very much to hear from our author that he had dictated to a pupil of his, while instructing him in the Philosophy of Descartes, the whole of the Second Part, and a portion of the Third Part, demonstrated in the geometrical manner, also some of the more important and difficult questions, usually discussed in Metaphysics, which Descartes had not yet disentangled ; and that he had acceded to the persistent entreaties and pressure of his friends to publish these with his corrections and additions. Thereupon I also approved this plan, and at the same time readily offered my help, in case he should need it in connection with the publication. Moreover, I begged and persuaded him to put also the First Part of the Principles into a similar form and to put it before the others, so that the whole thing, arranged in this manner, may from its beginning be at once more intelligible and more pleasing. Seeing that this was very reasonable, he would not disregard the entreaties of a friend or the advantage of the reader ; and he entrusted to my care the whole business of printing and publishing, as he is living in the country far from town, and so can not be here.

These, then, are the things that we give you, fair reader, in this little book : namely, the First and Second Parts of René Descartes's Principles of Philosophy, with a fragment of the Third Part, and to these we have added, under the name of an Appendix, the Metaphysical Thoughts of our Author. But as to " the first part of the Principles," although we use the expression here and the title of the little book puts it before us, we would not have it understood as though everything which Descartes has said there, were set out here demonstrated in geometrical manner ; the designation has only been taken from what is more important in it, so that only the chief problems which concern Metaphysics, and which Descartes treated in his Meditations, have been selected (all other matters, which are of logical interest and only narrated or surveyed as a matter of history, are omitted). Indeed, in order to accomplish these things more easily, the author has copied *verbatim* almost everything that Descartes has expressed in geometrical manner near the end of his *Answer to the Second Objections* ; so that all his Definitions are set out first, and his Propositions are inserted among the author's, but the Axioms are not put immediately after the Definitions, but are inserted only after the fourth Proposition, and their order is changed to facilitate their proof, and some things which were not necessary have been omitted. And although it did not escape our author that these Axioms (as Descartes himself shows in the case of Postulate 7) can be demonstrated like Theorems, and can even come more suitably under the name of Propositions, and although we even besought him to do it so, yet the greater occupations in which he is immersed only allowed him two weeks' leisure, in which he was compelled to finish this work, and so could not satisfy his own or our desire, but he added a brief, connecting explanation which may serve as a substitute for a demonstration, and put off till another time a fuller edition dealing with all the parts, if perchance after this hustled edition a new one be prepared. For such an augmented edition I will endeavour to persuade him to complete the whole of the Third Part on the Visible World (of which we only add a fragment, as the author ended his exposition at this point, and we would not deprive the reader of it, small though it is). And in order that this may be carried out as it should be, certain Propositions concerning the nature and properties of Fluids will be inserted here and there in the Second Part ; and I will make every endeavour to persuade the author to carry this out, when the time comes.

Our Author diverges from Descartes very often not only in the formulations and explanations of the Axioms, but even as regards his proofs of the Propositions themselves and the remaining Conclusions, and uses a kind of Demonstration which is very different from that of Descartes. Let no one, however, so interpret this as if the Author wished to correct that most distinguished Man in these matters ; let him rather think of the author as doing this for the sole purpose of being able to retain the better the order which he had already adopted, and so as not to increase unduly the number of Axioms. For the same reason he was also compelled to prove many things which Descartes set down without any proof, and to add what he has entirely omitted.

Above all, however, I would remark that in all these, namely, in the First and Second Parts of the Principles, in the fragment of the Third Part, as also in his Metaphysical Thoughts, our Author has set down Descartes's real thoughts and their proofs, as they are found in his writings, or as they ought to be deduced by valid reasoning from the fundamental principles laid down by him. For after he had promised to teach his pupil the philosophy of Descartes it was his sacred duty not to diverge from his thought by a finger's breadth, or to dictate anything that either did not correspond with his doctrines or was opposed to them. On this account, let no one think that he teaches here either his own views or only such as he approves. For although he regards some of them as true, and admits that he has added some views of his own, yet there are many views here which he rejects as false, favouring a view very different from them. An instance of this sort among others, to bring forward but one case out of many, is the statement about the Will in the *Scholium to Proposition 15*, in the *First Part of the Principles*, and in chapter 12, *Part II. of the Appendix*, although the proofs appear to be given with sufficiently great pains and care. For he does not think that the Will is distinct from the Intellect, much less that it is endowed with such freedom. For in making these assertions Descartes, as appears from the *Essay on Method, Part 4, and Meditations 2,* and other places, merely assumes, but does not prove, that the human mind is an absolute thinking substance. On the other hand, although our Author admits indeed that there is a thinking substance in Nature, yet he denies that it constitutes the essence of the human mind ; but he maintains that just as extension is limited by no boundaries, so Thought likewise is limited by no boundaries ; so that, in the same way as the human Body is not absolute extension, but only limited in a certain mode by motion and rest according to the laws of extended Nature, so likewise the human Mind or Spirit is not absolute thought, but only limited by ideas in a certain mode according to the laws of thinking Nature ; and these, he concludes, are necessarily given when the human body begins to exist. From this Definition, he thinks, it is not difficult to prove that the Will is not distinct from the Intellect, much less that it is capable of the freedom which Descartes ascribes to it ; but that even the very power of affirming and denying is absolutely fictitious ; for affirming and denying are nothing apart from the ideas ; that the remaining faculties, such as Intellect, Desire, etc., ought to be included among the figments or those notions which men have formed by con-

152

ceiving things abstractly, such notions are those of humanity, lapidity, and others of the same kind.

Mention must also be made of the fact that the expression, found in several places, that *this or that is beyond human comprehension*, ought to be received in the same way, that is, as expressing only the mind of Descartes. For it must not be taken to mean that our Author makes such utterances the expressions of his own thought. For he holds that all those things, and even many others more sublime and subtle, can not only be conceived by us clearly and distinctly, but can even be easily explained, if only the human Intellect be led to the search for truth and the Knowledge of things along another path than that which was cleared and made smooth by Descartes ; and the foundations of the sciences as laid by Descartes, and all that he himself has constructed upon them, are not sufficient to disentangle and solve all the difficult questions which are met with in Metaphysics, but others are required if we desire to uplift our intellect to that summit of Knowledge.

Lastly (to bring the preface to an end) we wish the Readers to know that all these treatises are published for no other purpose than that of discovering and spreading the truth, and in order to persuade men to turn to the study of true and genuine Philosophy.

.   .   .   .   .

§ 3. *From Jarig Jelles's Preface to the " Post-humous Works " of Spinoza* (1677).

From an early age he was nourished on books, and in his youth he studied Theology for many years ; but after he had reached the age when the mind matures and becomes competent to investigate the nature of things, he devoted himself whole-heartedly to philosophy. As, however, neither the teachers of these studies, nor those who have written about them, gave him the information he wanted, and he was aglow with the highest love of Knowledge, he decided to find out for himself what strength of mind might achieve in these things. In the pursuit of this plan the philosophical writings of that most distinguished and greatest philosopher, René Descartes, were of great service to him. After freeing himself from all kinds of occupations and the cares of business affairs, which to a large extent are an obstacle to the search for truth, and in order to be less disturbed in his meditations by friends, he left the city of Amsterdam, in which he was born and brought up, and took

154

up his abode first in Rhynsburg, then in Voorburg, and finally in the Hague, where he died of phthisis on February 21, 1677, after completing his 44th year of age. He did not devote himself entirely to the search for truth only, but he also occupied himself with Optics and with grinding and polishing lenses that could be used for Telescopes and Microscopes ; and if an untimely death had not snatched him away, achievements of outstanding merit might have been expected of him (for he showed sufficiently what he could accomplish in these things). Although indeed he withdrew himself entirely from the world and hid himself, yet, owing to his solid erudition and his great mental acumen, he became known to a great many men distinguished for their learning and eminence : as may be seen from the letters written to him, and his replies to them.

He spent most of his time in investigating the nature of things, in reducing discoveries to order, and in communicating them to his friends ; very little of his time was spent in mental recreation. Such ardour for the pursuit of truth was burning within him that, according to the testimony of those with whom he lodged, for three successive months he would not go out into the open. Indeed, lest he be disturbed in his search for truth, and that he might rather proceed with it according to his own wish, he even declined modestly a professorship in the Heidelberg Academy, offered to him by His Serene Highness, the Elector Palatine, as is evident from his 53rd and 54th letter. [Now Letters 47 and 48.]

From this devotion to truth and his immense diligence there came forth in the year 1664 [1663] *René Descartes's Principles of Philosophy, Parts I and II, Demonstrated Geometrically* by our author, and appended to it were his *Metaphysical Thoughts*; in 1670, moreover, the *Tractatus Theologico-Politicus*, in which are treated things most subtle and most worthy of consideration in respect of Theology, Holy Scripture, and the true and solid foundations of the Commonwealth.

From the same fountain there flowed what are here presented to the Reader under the title *B. D. S. Posthumous Works*; but these are all that could be collected from note-books and certain copies which were hidden away among his friends and acquaintances. And although it is believable that some work of our philosopher not found here may still lie hidden away with this man or that, yet it is thought nevertheless that nothing will be found in it that has not already been said more than once in these writings; except perchance it be the small *Treatise on the Rainbow* which, as is known to some people, he composed several years ago, and which lies hidden somewhere, unless, as is probable, he consigned it to the fire.

The name of the author is indicated on the front page of the book and elsewhere by the initial letters only, for no other reason than that shortly before his death he asked explicitly that his name should not figure on his *Ethics*, which he ordered to be printed ; but the reason for the prohibition appears to be no other than that he did not want his teaching to derive its name from him. For he says in the Appendix to the Fourth Part of his *Ethics*, Section 25, that " those who desire to help others with advice or service, so that these may likewise enjoy the highest good, will least of all seek that their teaching should bear their own name " ; moreover, in the Third Part of his *Ethics*, in Definition 44 of the Feelings, where he explains what ambition is, he explicitly charges those who do this kind of thing with a desire for Glory.

Now, with regard to these writings of his, the *Ethics*, although the preface to Part I is wanting, is, nevertheless, a long way ahead of the others, and can be regarded as an independent and complete work. . . .

.   .   .   .   .

The *Political Treatise* our author composed shortly before his death. Its ideas are carefully developed and its style is clear. Here he leaves aside the opinions of many politicians, and sets out his own views in the most thorough fashion, deducing all kinds of conclusions from his presuppositions. . . . His untimely death was the reason why he did not finish this Treatise, and why he did not treat of Laws nor of various questions relating to politics, as may be seen from the author's letter to a friend, which preceded the *Political Treatise*.

The *Treatise on the Improvement of the Understanding* belongs to the earliest works of our philosopher, as is shown by its style and ideas. The dignity of the subject which he treats therein, and the great service which he set before himself as its end, namely, to prepare the easiest and smoothest way to the true Knowledge of things, always spurred him on to complete it. But the amount of work, the deep meditations, and the vast knowledge of things which were needed to complete it, only allowed it to proceed at a slow pace, and were the reason why it was not finished, and why here and there something is missing. For in the notes which he himself added, the author frequently points out that what he is considering there is to be demonstrated more carefully, or explained more fully, either in his Philosophy or elsewhere.

.   .   .   .   .

. . . All these works, with the exception of a few letters, were written in Latin.

.   .   .   .   .

It was always his intention to publish a Hebrew Grammar demonstrated in the geometrical method, in the preface to which he would have shown that the correct pronunciation of this language had long ceased to be known. . . .

.   .   .   .   .

All who sincerely love Truth and strive after a solid and indisputable Knowledge of things, will, beyond a doubt, feel the greatest grief that these writings of our philosopher are in great part incomplete. It is certainly to be lamented that one who had already made such advances in the knowledge of truth and who had acquired for himself so much ability to make further progress in it, should have met with his death so prematurely, so untimely ; all the more so as not only the completion of these writings but even a whole Philosophy might have been expected, which he refers to in various places in the *Treatise on the Improvement of the Understanding,*

159

and in which, no doubt, he would have demonstrated the true nature of motion, and by what a priori reasoning the many variations in Matter might be deduced, to which reference is made in Letters 73 and 74. [Now 59 and 60.]

He also proposed to himself to write an Algebra in a more concise and more intelligible manner, also many other works, as various of his friends heard him say many times. But death shows also in the case of our very acute philosopher that what men propose is seldom carried out.

§ 4. *From Pierre Bayle's " Historical and Critical Dictionary " (1697, 1702).*

. . . As he had a geometrical mind, and as he wanted to find a reason for everything, he soon perceived that the teaching of the Rabbis was not for him : so much so that it was readily observed that he disapproved of Judaism in respect of many of its articles of faith ; for he was a man who did not like any constraint on conscience, and he was a great enemy of dissimulation ; hence he declared freely his doubts and his belief. It is said that the Jews offered to tolerate him, if only he would outwardly conform to their rites, and that they even promised him a yearly pension ; but that he could not

reconcile himself to such hypocrisy. Nevertheless, he only withdrew from their Synagogue
gradually, and maybe he would to some extent
have long continued to show regard for them,
if he had not been treacherously attacked, on
leaving the theatre, by a Jew who stabbed him
with a knife. The wound was slight, but he
believed that it was the assassin's intention to
kill him. After that he entirely severed his
connection with them, and that was why they
excommunicated him. I have investigated into
the circumstances, but have not succeeded in
unearthing them. He composed in Spanish
an Apology for his exit from the Synagogue.
This writing has not been printed ; it is known,
however, that he put into it many of the things
which appeared subsequently in his *Tractatus
Theologico-Politicus*, printed in Amsterdam in the
year 1670. . . . When Spinoza devoted himself
to philosophical studies, he soon lost all taste
for the ordinary systems, and found wonderful
satisfaction in that of Mr. Descartes. . . . His
life of retirement did not prevent the spread of
his name and fame. Free-thinkers hastened
to him from all parts (Edition 1697, vol. ii,
pp. 1085-1088).

The late Prince Condé, who was almost as learned as he was brave, and who did not dislike intercourse with free-thinkers, wanted to see Spinoza, and provided him with the necessary passports for the journey to Utrecht. At the time he was in command of the French troops there. I have heard it said that he was obliged to visit some place on the very day that Spinoza was due to arrive, and that the period of the passport expired before the Prince returned to Utrecht, so that he did not see the philosopher and author of the *Tractatus Theologico-Politicus* ; but he had given orders that in his absence a very good reception should be given to Spinoza, and that they should not let him depart without a present. The author of the Reply to the Religion of the Hollanders speaks about it in this manner *:
" Before quitting this chapter I must make known my astonishment on seeing that Stoupe wanted so much to declaim against Spinoza, and that he says that there are many in this country who visit him, seeing that, during his stay in Utrecht, he himself formed and cultivated such a close friendship with him. For I am assured that, at his request, Prince Condé brought him from the Hague to Utrecht for the express purpose of conversing with him, and that Stoupe had

* Brun : *The Real Religion of the Hollanders,* p. 164.

praised him warmly and had lived very intimately with him." (Edition 1697, vol. ii, p. 1088, Note F.)

. . . . .

Those who associated with Spinoza, and the peasants in the villages in which he lived for some time in retirement, are unanimous in saying that he was a man it was good to associate with, affable, honest, obliging, and very correct in his morals. This is strange ; but at bottom it is not more astonishing than it is to see people who live very immorally although they are fully persuaded of the truth of the Gospel. (*Ibid.*, p. 1088.)

. . . . .

It is not true that his followers are numerous. Very few people are suspected of adhering to his doctrine ; and among those who are so suspected, there are few who have studied it ; and among these there are few who have grasped it, and who have not been repelled by the obstacles and impenetrable abstractions which they encounter therein. But so it is : *prima facie* all are called Spinozists who have no religion, and who make no great secret of it. Just so in France all are called Socinians who are regarded as unbelievers in the mysteries of the Gospel, although most

163

of these people have never read Socinius or his disciples. (*Ibid.*, p. 1100.)

.   .   .   .   .

A certain Jarig Jelles, his intimate friend, being suspected of some heresies, thought that he ought to justify himself by publishing a confession of his faith. Having drafted it, he sent it to Spinoza, and asked him to write his opinion of it. Spinoza replied to him that he had read it with pleasure, and that he had not found anything in it which could be altered. " Sir and very distinguished Friend : Your writings which have been sent to me I have read through with pleasure, and found them such that I can change nothing in them." This confession of faith is in Dutch and was printed in the year 1684.*
(Edition 1702, vol. iii, p. 2783, Note S.)

§ 5. *From Sebastian Kortholt's Preface to Christian Kortholt's Book, " On Three Great Impostors "* (1700).

About Spinosa, the very celebrated Pierre Bayle † has written since the time of my Father.

* In Amsterdam. The title is as follows : *Confession of the Universal and Christian Faith contained in a letter to N. N. by Jarig Jelles.*

† *Historical and Critical Dictionary*, Rotterdam, 1697, vol. ii, pp. 1083 to 1100.

He has reported more fully about Spinosa's life, writings and opponents than did the editor of his posthumous works, seeing that he only touched briefly on his mode of life. If I add to these some few little known and hitherto unpublished facts, I trust that I shall be doing something not unwelcome to the Benevolent Reader. But I will add nothing except what I personally gathered, some years ago, when I was staying in the Hague, from well-informed and trustworthy men, above all from the members of Spinosa's household, and his landlord, H. van der S. . . . a very trustworthy man and an extremely artistic painter, who had actually portrayed the face of the Atheist. According to these witnesses Benedict Spinosa was the son of a Jewish merchant in Amsterdam, and was called Baruch. In his boyhood already he aroused his father's great dislike against him because, although destined for commerce, he devoted himself entirely to letters. The Latin language he learned with avidity under the guidance and auspices of a learned young woman, together with Mr. Kerck . . . of Hamb., a pupil whom the Teacher afterwards married. On his father's death he left his native city, leaving the whole of his inheritance (with the exception of one bed only) to his kin. Yet he never left the Netherlands ;

but betook himself first to Rhynsburg, then to Voorburg, and lastly to the Hague, where the said H. van der S. provided him with board and lodging, and where he lived an extremely lonely life. It is certainly very true, as is related by the editor of the Atheist's posthumous works, that he stayed at home for several whole months at a time. For, being much too diligent, he devoted himself to his studies far into the night, and for the most part toiled over his dark writings by lamplight from the tenth evening hour until the third, and mostly abstained from human intercourse in the daytime, so that not an hour be lost for the work of his own undoing, and the perdition of others. The accuracy of this is confirmed by what Mr. Christ. Nic. von Greiffencrantz, Councillor to His Serene Highness the Duke of Holstein, and who associated with Spinosa in the Hague in the seventy-second year of this century [1672], said about him in his letter sent to my Father on the 6th April, 1681, from Holm in Sweden : *he seemed*, says he, *to live all to himself, always lonely, and as if buried in his study.* Seneca would, accordingly, have said of Spinosa what he said of Servelius Vatia when passing by the villa in which he was always hidden away as in a grave : *Vatia lies buried here.* Sometimes, however, he sought mental recreation

166

by polishing lenses which his landlord actually showed me as things worth seeing, together with some pictures executed by the same hand : and occasionally he found leisure for learned and distinguished men, whom he allowed entry rather than went out of his way to meet, and with whom he carried on conversations about civic affairs. He referred to the name of a Politician, and in his mind and with his Knowledge he shrewdly foresaw future events, which he not infrequently foretold to his hosts. Jews he did not always exclude from his home, and he devoted some of his time to pupils whom he infected free of charge with the evil of his opinions. For he was a bad Atheist gratuitously. He professed himself, however, a Christian, and not only himself attended meetings of Reformers or of Lutherans, but frequently urged and exhorted others to frequent places of worship, and very strongly commended to the members of his household certain preachers of the gospel. Never did an oath or a frivolous remark about God pass the lips of Spinosa ; nor did he indulge in much wine, but lived a rather rigorous life. So he only paid his landlord 80 Dutch guilders quarterly, and spent at most 400 a year. He had entirely no desire for money, otherwise, [that is, if he were] a man craving for fame and were

167

more ambitious, he would not have refused several times the post of a Professor which had been offered him, or more proudly he might have chosen to be cruelly torn to pieces with his friends the De Witts if for a short life he would get an eternity of glory. For when he had completed his forty-fourth year, and had scarcely lived six years with the said painter, the Philosopher, exhausted from night-work, became ill. Yet he thought always of life, was unmindful of imminent death, and on February 21, 1677, he said to his landlord, who was going to hear a preacher in the afternoon, " God willing, we shall resume our conversation after the sermon." But before his host returned home he gave up his impure soul and breathed his last breath peacefully in the presence of only a Doctor of Medicine from Amsterdam. Whether such a death can fall to the lot of an Atheist, was not long ago the subject of discussion among learned men. After Spinosa's death many learned men, among them Cl. Bontekoë, tried very hard to acquire the books which he left. But like Hobbes he attached no great importance to a large store of books, and left scarcely forty, which the learned competed for at a very high price. Among them was not found the *Treatise on the Rainbow*, which Spinosa had written with great pains, and which the

Editor of the posthumous works thinks may perchance even now lie hidden somewhere.* But on the other hand I have it as certain that the author, in the year of his death, consigned a book not to the [candle] flame but to the fire, on the same day on which nearly all the processions through the streets in the Hague were illuminated with festive fires ; whereat he remarked jestingly that he was imitating those merry flashes and producing at home merriment and festive flames, adding : " I have devoted prolonged and much study to the thinking out and writing down of things which now certainly no one will read." O would that he had likewise consigned to the avenging flames his remaining works, which cast shadows over the light of the clearest truth, products of an errant phantasy, and most horrid spectres of the horned portal, which should have been relegated to hell, whence they had come, so that they might not land anyone who reads them in flames that can never be extinguished ! But in order that he should not cease to do harm even after his death, he entrusted, on the day before he died, the books written by his hand to the care of his landlord, who had warned him of his mortality, so that they might be transmitted to Joh. Riversenius, an Amsterdam

* See Preface to *B. D. S. Posthumous Works*, 1677, 4°.

bookseller. This was done, and in the same year the Posthumous Works came into people's hands, and gave rise among them to different opinions, though all intelligent men judged them to be discordant and impious beyond measure.

VII

ANNOTATIONS

ANNOTATIONS

PAGE 40.

As a matter of fact there are several portraits of Spinoza. The best of them is the one in the Library at Wolfenbüttel. See *Frontispiece*.

PAGE 42.

Baruch means *Blessed*, so does *Benedictus*. For many centuries it was customary among scholars to Latinize their names, e.g., *Agricola* for Bauer (= Peasant), *de Sacrobosco* for Holywood.

.   .   .   .   .

The father of Spinoza, Michael de Espinoza, came from Figueira in South Portugal, and appears to have been a merchant of some standing. He lived in a substantial house in Amsterdam, and held various offices in the Jewish community there.

The idea that Spinoza took up the study of Hebrew Literature because his father could not set him up in business is erroneous. Then and long afterwards every young Jew would study Hebrew Literature for several years whatever his subsequent career.

PAGE 43.

That Spinoza *read and re-read the Talmud* is improbable. The Talmud with its commentaries when printed in legible type occupy twelve folio volumes ; without the commentaries, say, two such volumes. A great deal of its contents would have no interest for Spinoza. But no doubt he had read and re-read certain of its more interesting portions, such as *The Ethics of the Fathers.*

PAGE 44.

SAUL MORTEIRA was born in Venice in 1596. He studied medicine under Montalto, Court Physician of Maria de Medici. Montalto was a Marano, that is outwardly a Christian of necessity, but a Jew at heart. In 1616 Montalto died suddenly while accompanying Louis XIII to Tours. His body was taken by Saul Morteira to Amsterdam for burial in the recently acquired Jewish cemetery at Ouwerkerk (also called Ouderkerk), near that city. While in Amsterdam on this pious errand Morteira received and accepted a call to the Rabbinate of the older of the two synagogues there (the *House of Jacob*). A third synagogue was established in 1618. But in 1638 the three synagogues were united, and Morteira acted as the senior or presiding

174

Rabbi. He had had a taste of Court life, and was not entirely lacking in philosophical appreciation ; but may have been rather autocratic and narrow. He died in Amsterdam in 1660.

Page 45.

Angels. The Hebrew word for *angels* really means *messengers*.

Page 46.

The Old Testament lays little if any stress on immortality in order to discourage the worship of the dead, a practice greatly in vogue among the ancients.

Page 50.

Chief of the Synagogue is not a correct description. He was the presiding Rabbi when the Rabbis conferred about Jewish matters.

. . . . .

The account of Spinoza's cheeky answer here and on page 51 does not ring true.

Page 51.

Spinoza associated with Christians, and commenced the study of Latin, long before his excommunication.

PAGE 52.

If any language can be called Spinoza's "natural language" or mother-tongue it was Spanish. Spanish was the language in which he was taught the Jewish religion and literature at school ; it was the language in which he was excommunicated, and in which he wrote his *Defence*, or *Apology*.

. . . . .

VAN DEN ENDEN is undoubtedly the correct name. How Codex Towneley came to the name Van den *Hebden* is difficult to explain, except perhaps on the assumption that the passage was read out to the copyist by someone who had a cold at the time.

. . . . .

FRANCISCUS AFFINIUS VAN DEN ENDEN was born in Antwerp in 1600. He studied Letters, Law and Medicine in the University of Löwen, where he was offered a professorship at eighteen. For a time he was a Jesuit, but left that Order, and married about 1642. About 1645 he moved to Amsterdam, and appears to have been sent on a secret political mission to Madrid. In 1650 or thereabouts he opened a bookshop in Amsterdam, but was not successful. So he opened a

176

school about 1652, specializing in the Classical languages and in the " new philosophy." He was assisted by his oldest daughter Clara Maria, who was somewhat deformed physically but exceptionally intelligent. In 1657 his pupils gave public performances in the theatre of a play by Terence and of another written by Van den Enden himself. Mr. and Mrs. Grundy did their worst to prevent these performances, but in vain. Other plays were staged again in 1658. Was it on one of these occasions that Spinoza was attacked by a fanatical Jew ?

In 1671 Van den Enden moved to Paris, where he opened a school in one of the suburbs. In 1674 a conspiracy was organized against Louis XIV. It was headed by De Rohan, De Préault, and the Marquise De Villars. In some way Van den Enden was drawn into it, and acted as intermediary with the Dutch, who were to attack the port of Quillebeuf and help to start a revolution in Normandy. It was arranged that a certain innocent-looking announcement in the *Gazette d'Hollande* should serve as a signal for the movements to begin. But the conspiracy collapsed, and the conspirators were imprisoned in the Bastille, and then executed. Such was the tragic end of Van den Enden, who deserved a better fate.

PAGE 52.

The description of the excommunication is taken from some picturesque story-teller. A note in the Le Vier edition refers to Seldenus : *On the Law of Nature and of Nations* (see *Annotation* to p. 105). The plain story is translated on pages 145–147.

PAGE 56.

The Le Vier edition inserts the following remark after the word " Rabbi " in the top line :

" So true is it that the clergy, no matter what their religion may be, be they Heathens, Jews, Christians, Mohammedans, are more zealous about their own Authority than about Justice and Truth, and that they are all alike animated with the spirit of Persecution."

．　　．　　．　　．　　．

After his expulsion in 1656, Spinoza went for a few months to Ouwerkerk, a village near Amsterdam, to which city he then returned. He did not move to Rhynsburg until 1660, and then stayed there until 1663. Rhynsburg is a village near Leyden. The cottage in which Spinoza lived there is now a Spinoza Museum.

178

ANNOTATIONS

PAGE 57.

Here we are told one reason for the publication of Spinoza's version of Descartes's *Principia*. Another is given in L. Meyer's Preface to the book (see pp. 147 ff.), and yet a third reason is given by Spinoza in *Letter* XIII (old IX). The book was published in 1663, and a Dutch translation in 1664. Hence the confusion.

PAGE 58.

Voorburg is a village near the Hague. Spinoza lived here from 1663 till 1670, when he moved to the Hague.

PAGE 60.

Spinoza was offered the Heidelberg Professorship in 1673.

PAGE 61.

Note (8). A footnote in the Le Vier edition points out that these comments are not in any of the Latin editions, but only in the French translation of the *Tractatus Theologico-Politicus*.

PAGE 62.

The real reason why Spinoza accepted Condé's invitation to Utrecht was because he and those whom he consulted hoped that he might help to end the war between France and Holland.

PAGE 65.

MURDER OF THE DE WITTS. Leibniz reports as follows : " After dinner I spent several hours with Spinoza. He told me that on the day of the murder of the De Witts he felt impelled to go out in the evening and exhibit in the neighbourhood of the crime a poster with the words ' Lowest Barbarians ! ' But his landlord had locked the door to prevent his going out and incurring the risk of being torn to pieces " (Foucher de Careil : *Réfutation inédite de Spinoza par Leibniz*, p. lxiv). Leibniz visited Spinoza in 1676.

PAGE 70.

Note (12). *Theophrastus* is an error. In the passage referred to (*Anot. ad Nov. Test.* p. 433 of ed. 1542) Erasmus mentions *Theophylaktos*.

PAGE 74.

Probably an allusion to Aristotle, who fled from Athens in order to save his enemies from repeating the crime committed against Socrates.

PAGE 79.

The *Advertisement* and the *Preface of the Copyist* are contained in the Halle copy, but not in the London copy of the Le Vier edition of 1719.

And there is no sign of these pages having been removed from the London copy. What is the explanation ? I suggest that the first copies were printed and sold without the *Avertissement* and *Préface du Copiste*, and that it was only after an outcry had been raised against the book that these additions were made to the remaining copies, in the hope of saving them and those responsible for them. If the editor had really intended from the beginning to include these specious apologies, he would not have put on the very title-page those flattering rhymes about Spinoza, which make the insincerity of the Apology too palpable. The title-page of the 1735 re-issue does not contain the rhymes ; and the removal of the provoking rhymes, I believe, was probably the principal reason for having a new title-page.

PAGE 83.

The view expressed in the Le Vier edition is correct. Some copies have all three title-pages.

PAGE 85.

SIMON JOOSTEN DE VRIES. The account in the Le Vier text is based on Colerus's *Life of Spinoza*, Chapter 9, near the end.

De Vries was an Amsterdam merchant who studied under the direction of Spinoza. He was about a year younger than his teacher. His regard for Spinoza is evident from his letter written in 1663 to Rhynsburg : " For a long time," he wrote, " I have been longing to be with you ; but the weather and the hard winter have not been propitious to me. Sometimes I complain of my lot in being removed from you by a distance which separates us so much. Happy, most happy is your companion Casearius, who lives with you under the same roof, and who can converse with you about the most excellent topics during dinner, or supper, or on your walks. But although we are so far apart in the body, yet you have constantly been present to my mind, especially when I take your writings in my hand, and apply myself to them." De Vries, Jelles and others formed a reading circle to whom Spinoza sent his *Short Treatise*, etc., in manuscript for study and criticism. De Vries died in 1667.

PAGE 88.

JAN H. GLAZEMAKER translated some of the ancient classics and nearly all the works of Descartes into Dutch. He also translated most of Spinoza's works, namely the *Tractatus Theo-*

logico-Politicus, and all the *Opera Posthuma* except the *Hebrew Grammar* (see p. 188 f.). The Dutch translation of Spinoza's version of Descartes's *Principia* was made by Pieter Balling, a friend of Spinoza.

. . . . .

PERROT D'ABLANCOURT (1606–1664) translated many of the classics (Cæsar, Lucian, Tacitus, Thucydides, etc.) into French.

PAGE 105.

L'Excommunication.—The Le Vier edition has the following note :

" On trouvera dans la Traité de Seldenus, *De Jure Naturæ et Gentium*, la Formulaire de l'Excommunication ordinaire dont les *Juifs* se servent pour retrancher de leur corps les violateurs de leur Loy."

PAGE 110.

Un de ses amis. To this there is the following note in the Le Vier edition :

" Cet ami est Mr. Louis Meyer, Médécin d'Amsterdam."

. . . . .

To footnote (5) the Le Vier edition adds : "Apud Johan. Riewerts, 1663," which is a correction of the text.

PAGE III.

Voorburg. "Village à une lieuë de *Haye.*" Note in the Le Vier edition.

PAGE 112.

Heidelberg. The Le Vier edition adds this note :

"Charles Louis, Electeur Palatin, lui fit offrir une Chaire de Professeur en Philosophie à Heydelbergh, avec une très ample liberté de philosopher ; mais il remercia S. A. E. avec beaucoup de Politesse."

PAGE 113.

Footnote (8). Instead of this the Le Vier edition has the following note :

"Ces éclaircissements ont été traduits en François et se trouvent à la fin de la *Clef du Sanctuaire.* Ils ne sont dans aucune Edition Latine de ce Livre. Il y en a deux, l'une in 4, comme nous l'avons marqué dans la Note précédente, et l'autre 8, à laquelle est joint le Traité intitulé *Philosophia S. Scripturae Interpres,* dont on prétend que Mr. Louis Meyer est Autheur. Ces deux Traitez sont mis sous ce Titre, *Danielis Hensii Operum Historicorum collectio*, Pars 1 et 2. 8°. Ludg. Bat. 1673."

PAGE 147.

LODEWIJK MEYER was born in Amsterdam, in 1630, of Lutheran parents. From an early age he entertained poetic ambitions, and wrote a considerable amount of verse on various topics. In course of time he also wrote some plays. But he was not above doing more humdrum, though perhaps more useful work. Already at the age of twenty he published a small book explaining some 3,600 foreign terms used in Holland. He did not write it all himself, but his share was considerable. It went through several editions, enlarged each time. In 1654 he entered the University of Leyden, where he first studied philosophy, and later on medicine. Meyer probably met Spinoza in the house of Van den Enden. Meyer's daughters attended Van den Enden's school and took part in the *Medea* in 1664. In 1663 Meyer wrote the Preface to Spinoza's geometric version of Descartes's *Principia*, and saw the work through the press. In 1665 he became the Director of the Amsterdam Theatre, but still found time for philosophy. In 1666 he published his book

Philosophy the Interpreter of Holy Scripture, which contains some allusions to Spinoza. In 1669 Meyer ceased to be Director of the Theatre, and founded soon afterwards a Society of Arts which had for its motto : *Nil volentibus arduum* (" Where there is a will there is a way "). In 1677 he resumed control over the Theatre. He died in 1681. It is the opinion of Meinsma that the best of the existing portraits of Spinoza, which is now in the Library at Wolfenbüttel, belonged to Meyer originally. It was bought from the executors of Professor Francius, who was Meyer's co-Director of the Amsterdam Theatre. (The frontispiece of this book is a reproduction of the Wolfenbüttel portrait.)

PAGE 147.

The pupil whom Spinoza taught the philosophy of Descartes was Casearius.

· · · · ·

JOHANNES CASEARIUS was born in 1642, and was probably a pupil in Van den Enden's school in Amsterdam. In 1661 he entered the University of Leyden, and sometime afterwards went to live in Rhynsburg, where he stayed in the same cottage as Spinoza and received instruction from him in the new (i.e. Cartesian) philosophy. Some of the more enterprising undergraduates at Leyden used to visit Rhynsburg (which is near Leyden) to attend the Collegiant meetings there. Casearius may have met Spinoza in that way, or he may have known him from Van den Enden's school, where Spinoza had taught for a time. Casearius appears to have caused Spinoza some anxiety during those Rhynsburg days, being rather superficial, and addicted to novelty rather than devoted to truth ; but Spinoza confidently expected better things of him when he matured (see Spinoza's Letter to De Vries, 1663, No. IX.). In 1665 Casearius was ordained by the Reformed Church in Amsterdam. In 1668 he was appointed to a post in the Dutch East Indies. Eventually he ministered to the Christian souls in Malabar. Here he came into contact with Van Reede, the Governor, who took a deep interest in Botany, and published eventually his *Hortus Malabaricus*. The text of the first two folio volumes of this once famous work was written by Casearius. He died in June 1677 of dysentery. In his Preface to vol. iii of the *Hortus Malabaricus* (1682) Van Reede paid a warm tribute to the memory of Casearius, whose name has since been given to a certain family of plants, the *Casearia*. Such in brief is the story of the pupil who was the occasion of Spinoza's first published work.

THE OLDEST BIOGRAPHY OF SPINOZA

PAGE 154.

JARIG JELLES was at one time a spice merchant in Amsterdam, but having a taste for study, and being in a position to indulge it, he handed over his business to a manager in 1653, and devoted the last thirty years of his life to the pursuit of Knowledge, which (according to the biographical introduction to his posthumous *Confession of Faith*) he found " better than choice gold." He was one of Spinoza's friends who persuaded him to publish his version of Descartes's *Principia*, and even defrayed the cost of its publication in 1663. When Spinoza's *Tractatus Theologico-Politicus* was published in 1670, Jan H. Glazemaker translated it into Dutch, probably at the request, or at least with the approval, of Jelles, but without Spinoza's knowledge. When Spinoza heard, in 1671 (from Prof. Graevius ?), of its impending appearance, he wrote to Jelles begging him to try to prevent its publication, as it would probably lead to the prohibition of the Latin original as well as of the translation. His wish was respected, and the translation was not published until 1693. According to a note written by Leibniz in 1676, Jelles was said to support Spinoza at the time. When Spinoza died in 1677 Jelles was one of the small band of friends who

188

took in hand the publication of the *Opera Post-huma*, to which he wrote the Preface. Glazemaker translated the Preface into Latin, and the *Opera Posthuma* (except the *Hebrew Grammar*) into Dutch. (According to one writer, it was Dr. L. Meyer who translated the Preface into Latin.) Jelles died in 1683. The following year saw the publication of his *Confession of Faith*, with a biographical introduction which assures the reader that Jelles " strove unremittingly to penetrate more and more deeply into the knowledge and love of God, and he made such progress therein that there are few people who have worked their way up to such a high level of spiritual insight."

.   .   .   .   .

It is remarkable that the Preface makes no allusion to Spinoza's Jewish origin. Some may see in this the usual tendency to credit the Jewish community with its bad specimen only. Others may infer from it what a sensible, good fellow Jelles must have been. Ludwig Börne once complained that some people disliked him because he was a Jew, others tolerated him in spite of his being a Jew, and yet others liked him just because of his being a Jew, but nobody ever forgot *that* he was a Jew. Perhaps Jelles was one of the rare exceptions who do not allow such differences to dull their perception of a common humanity.

PAGE 161.

The story of the attempted assassination of Spinoza is not mentioned in any work earlier than Bayle's account written in 1697, twenty years after Spinoza's death. The next reference to it is in Colerus (1705). According to Bayle it happened when Spinoza was leaving the theatre, according to Colerus Spinoza was leaving the synagogue at the time.

PAGE 164.

CHRISTIAN KORTHOLT (1633-1694) was Professor of Divinity at the University of Kiel. In 1680 he published a little book *De Tribus Impostoribus Magnis*, in which he undertook to show up Hobbes, Herbert of Cherbury, and Spinoza. The book was planned as a set-off against an older book in which Moses, Jesus, and Mohammed were described as *The Three Imposters*. In 1700 Sebastian Kortholt published a new edition of his father's book with a new Preface. It is difficult to say whether Sebastian was such an ass that he did not see that his facts contradicted his comments, or whether he wrote with his tongue in his cheek.

Page 165.

DIRCK (OR THEODOR) KERCKRINCK was born in Hamburg in 1639, and came with his parents to Amsterdam at an early age. At eighteen he suddenly decided to prepare for the University, and went to Van den Enden to learn Latin, etc., for the purpose. Two years later (1659) he entered the University of Leyden, and was still there when Spinoza came to Rhynsburg in 1660. Kerckrinck became a distinguished doctor, and some of his medical treatises are included in the inventory of Spinoza's books—no doubt gifts from an old friend whom he had met originally at Van den Enden's house. In 1671 Kerckrinck married Clara Maria, the eldest daughter of Van den Enden. Clara was twenty-seven then. Kerckrinck eventually settled in Hamburg, where he died in 1693.

Page 166.

Chr. N. Greiffencrantz was a German diplomatist. He represented the Duchy of Holstein at Vienna in 1688. Some of his correspondence with Leibniz is preserved in the Library at Hanover.

PAGE 168.

Cornelis Bontekoë was a Hague doctor.

. . . . .

The official inventory of Spinoza's estate enumerates, not 40, but 161 volumes. The text of the Inventory is given in Freudenthal's *Lebensgeschichte Spinozas*, pp. 158-165, and there is a French version of it in Van Rooyen's *Inventaire des Livres de Bénédict Spinoza*.

. . . . .

The *Treatise on the Rainbow* really turned out to have been stowed away by some friend of Spinoza. In 1680 it was published, together with an essay on the Calculation of Chances, by a bookseller named Levyn van Dyck. But it appears to have been lost sight of soon afterwards for many decades. About 1860 F. Muller, an Amsterdam bookseller, re-discovered it, and Van Vloten published it, together with the *Short Treatise*, etc., in his *Supplement* to Bruder's edition of Spinoza (1862).

INDEX

INDEX

194

INDEX

195

For Product Safety Concerns and Information please contact our EU
representative GPSR@taylorandfrancis.com
Taylor & Francis Verlag GmbH, Kaufingerstraße 24, 80331 München, Germany

www.ingramcontent.com/pod-product-compliance
Lightning Source LLC
Chambersburg PA
CBHW071409100726
47908CB00004B/1114